Albion Woodbury Small

The beginnings of American nationality

1774 to 1789

Albion Woodbury Small

The beginnings of American nationality
1774 to 1789

ISBN/EAN: 9783337150235

Printed in Europe, USA, Canada, Australia, Japan

Cover: Foto ©ninafisch / pixelio.de

More available books at **www.hansebooks.com**

THE BEGINNINGS

OF

AMERICAN NATIONALITY

JOHNS HOPKINS UNIVERSITY STUDIES

IN

HISTORICAL AND POLITICAL SCIENCE

HERBERT B. ADAMS, Editor.

History is past Politics and Politics present History — *Freeman.*

EIGHTH SERIES

I-II

THE BEGINNINGS

OF

AMERICAN NATIONALITY

The Constitutional Relations Between the Continental Congress and the Colonies and States from 1774 to 1789

BY ALBION W. SMALL, PH. D.

President of Colby University

BALTIMORE

PUBLICATION AGENCY OF THE JOHNS HOPKINS UNIVERSITY

January and February, 1890

TABLE OF CONTENTS.

The present number concludes with the introduction to Section VI. The next instalment of the work will continue the discussion through Chapters III and IV, or to the Declaration of Independence.

THE BEGINNINGS

OF

AMERICAN NATIONALITY.

CHAPTER I.

INTRODUCTION.

The facts of American history were very early confounded with the definitions and doctrines of a dogmatic political philosophy. Before our Constitution was three score years old, it had been associated with a mass of theoretical and fanciful folk lore, whose authenticity was more vehemently asserted than were the facts themselves. A body of tradition grew up about the origins of our nationality, and it became the mould in which all conclusions from documentary sources must be cast. This apocryphal element obscured the genuine portions of our history, and became the criterion by which events were judged, instead of remaining an hypothesis which the examination of evidence should justify or destroy.

The general view of our national development which found its ablest political champion in Daniel Webster, discovered in the history of the United States an experience absolutely unprecedented. It saw a nation "born in a day." It saw, nevertheless, the anomalous spectacle of repeatedly threatened and finally attempted self-destruction, in the body thus spontaneously generated. Persons who have approached the study

7

since the interpretation of our Constitution ceased to be a subject for angry dispute, are to be pardoned if they suspect that the point of observation from which our history presents such a phenomenal aspect was not fortunately chosen. It is not surprising that men who have been taught to trace between all historical causes and effects the slow procession of gradual advance, are suspicious of the alleged singular exception. They cannot silence the supposition that there must have been process and plan, not merely catastrophe, at the foundation of our nationality. They see no reason why, from material so abundant, compared with that by means of which so many remote periods have been revived, it should not be possible to reconstruct the plan of our national formation.

The men upon whom we have hitherto depended for a knowledge of our early constitutional history have embarrassed us with the abundance of their learning. Most conspicuously is this true of Mr. Bancroft. To depreciate his work would be no less uncritical than impertinent. Failure to regard him with grateful admiration would forcibly argue unfitness to be an apprentice where he is a master. Yet it may, without disrespect, be observed, that he has credited his readers with powers of discrimination which few possess. As a consequence, while performing a service beyond praise, he has imposed upon students a task which the majority will scarcely prove competent to perform.

It would be a labor of no mean merit to reorganize the material in Mr. Bancroft's last volumes, and arrange it in three groups, each exhibiting a distinct process of evolution. There is, in the first place, material in the volumes for a book on the development of individual opinion in America, upon political philosophy in general, and its particular application to the problems involved in the controversy with Great Britain. There is, in the second place, material for the history of that organization of political forces which was at length defined in the written Constitution of 1789. There is, finally, material for an account of that necessary assimilation of thought and feeling, without which written constitutions are simply words, a process which began with extreme provincialism, and which was going forward, not completed, in the adoption of the work of the Federal Convention. So long as these distinct lines of development are practically identified by students, so long will each and all of them be misunderstood. It is inevitable that the opinions of Washington and Jefferson and Hamilton upon public policy will seem to be indexes of general sentiment, and that they will color our interpretation of acts and enactments if all are presented together. If the significance of individual opinions is to be apprehended, the personal equation must be computed in every instance. This line of investigation can therefore be properly followed only by itself. If the political condition and development of the *masses* is to be exhibited, testimony of an entirely different sort must be adduced. Hence this must be a separate sphere of research and conclusion. If, finally, institutions are to be described, their action, not their definition, must be observed.

Failure to recognize these fundamental requirements is accountable for much that is misleading in attempts to expound our national experience.

It seems necessary, therefore, to draw, in the first place, very sharp lines between these different areas of investigation. This study is concerned, then, not with the growth of individual opinion, but with the growth of institutions. It is an effort to select a more natural vanishing point for the perspective of our national history.

The question proposed at the outset is :— *What was the exact relation of the Continental Congresses to the colonies and states.* Nearly all the fallacies in the literature of our constitutional history may be traced, wholly or in part, to *assumptions* in answer to this question. Our constitutional history cannot be written with authority until the question of fact

2

here raised is settled by appeal to the detailed evidence on record.[1]

The most natural method of exhibiting the relations between Congress and Colonies would seem to be, then, to place them before the reader in exactly the relations in which they appear in the public records. That method has been adopted in the following pages. After a brief account of the legal character of the communities with which the history deals, extracts from the records are arranged to show : *First*, the character of the bodies that assumed to act for the colonies ; *second*, the powers which these colonial bodies gave to representatives in the continental body ; *third*, the character of the continental body so composed ; *fourth*, the acts of the continental body ; *fifth*, the corresponding acts of the colonial bodies.

This method of exposition is applied *first*, to the period of the Congress of 1774; *second*, to that of the first session of the Congress of 1775; *third*, to that of the session September, 1775 to July, 1776; *fourth*, to the pre-confederation period, July, 1776 to March, 1781; *fifth*, to the period of the Confederation.

As hinted above, this study has proceeded upon the principle that in the nature of the case there is and can be but one text-book of our constitutional history. That book is in many parts, but it is composed solely of the authentic records of public acts, with occasionally admissible marginal notes drawn from more private sources. In collecting and arranging data for generalization from the public records, the exposition has gone forward as though these authorities had, up to

---

[1] It is astonishing that, after a space of thirty years for reflection, Mr. George Ticknor Curtis now reprints his history of the Constitution without revision of the assertions which beg this fundamental question. In the second chapter he repeats the dogma that the Congress of 1775 was a *"national government."* Until more exact analysis is applied, our early history must remain mythical.

the present, been unknown,[1] and as though no attempts had ever been made to describe our national development.

The second part will deal *first*, with the diplomacy of the Association and of the Confederation, as affecting nationality. No attempt to enter upon an exhaustive investigation of our diplomatic history is contemplated for the purposes of this inquiry, but an answer will be sought to the questions: What influence upon national formation was exerted by the fact that the associated and afterwards the confederated states acted practically as one nation in negotiating with foreign powers, in borrowing money, in sending and receiving ambassadors, and in concluding treaties? What effect of these proceedings can be traced in the development of a national consciousness and in the adoption of a national organization? Were the states in any way committed to nationality, as contrasted with alliance, by these foreign relations? It will be shown that while these relations logically *implied* nationality, the force of the logic was not admitted and enacted.

The second part will then discuss the relations between state and state within the Confederation. This is a necessary element in the view. The perspective could not have been so distorted if the details to be considered in this connection had not been unnoticed or unknown.[2]

The outcome of the study, up to 1789, is the demonstration that from this date two distinct questions were to be decided: 1. *What is the necessary legal interpretation of the Constitution on the subject of inter-state relations?* 2. Much more fundamental, but its importance was inadequately understood until

---

[1] As indeed to all intents and purposes they seem to have been to pretentious commentators upon our history, who might be named. Scores of faint and blurred composite photographs of many distant views are in circulation, purporting to be accurate representations of our institutions. The false impressions which these have created can only be effaced by studious attention to the clear and precise delineation of the records themselves.

[2] Portions of the evidence to be presented have been used in a popular way by Mr. John Fiske, in his *Critical Period of American History.*

it had passed into history—*What is the actual will of the people on the subject of inter-state relations?* The historian of the present generation, who studies the records independently, cannot fail to discover that while the logic of the Constitution answered the first question in one way, all the significant public acts of the period answered the second question in a contradictory way. The people of the United States simply dodged the responsibility of formulating their will upon the distinct subject of national sovereignty until the legislation of the sword began in 1861. The justification of the success of northern arms was not in its vindication of assertions about the meaning of events in 1775–89. It was in its proclamation of the completion of an historical process begun in 1775–89. This conclusion, which the documentary evidence irresistibly enforces, must determine the method of treating our history under the Constitution.[1]

To provide against rejection without a hearing, analysis of the facts thus to be reviewed, and criticism of the traditions and conventionalities founded upon them, must protest itself more patriotic than the inexact and illogical dogmatism which has claimed for these events a meaning that fastens an artificial construction upon our whole subsequent history. A precise estimate of the importance of these acts, as steps leading to governmental organization, does not diminish, but rather enhances, the value of each force and factor that contributed to the great completion. The exegesis which finds the transition from atomic colonial independence to organic nationality so easy that it is accomplished by a few resolutions, unwit-

---

[1] I plead guilty of the large ambition to follow out this method and rescue our constitutional history from the misinterpretations of Von Holst. The struggle of state sovereignty, in this country, for its right of primogeniture, and the gradual obliteration of that right through the development of new economic, social, and moral conditions, which at last violently prevailed, is a subject still obscure enough, but surely instructive enough to reward the labor of him who shall win recognition as its truthful historian.

tingly denies to the artificers of our Union the glory of great achievement. Confusion of distinctions whose discrimination measures and illustrates the length and difficulty of the progress from localism to nationality, instead of assuring to the men of the Revolution the fame they deserve, tends rather to the conclusion that obstacles so quickly overcome, and changes so spontaneously effected, were but factitious and trivial after all, and that consequently the evolution of nationality did not cost steadfastness and sacrifice and devotion especially memorable. If, on the other hand, nothing be interpreted into these acts which they did not literally contain; if steps be not magnified into strides, and strides into leaps; if foreshadowings be not confounded with actualities, and prophesies with fulfilments, the tremendous force of local inertia, resisting unification, can first be recognized and approximately estimated, and the splendid merit of converting a portion of this energy into national loyalty will then appear to belong not to a few, but to a succession of illustrious men, whose labors were crowned in the maturity of our nation, after a century of growth.

CHAPTER II.

THE CONGRESS OF 1774.

Section I. The Parties Represented.

Thirteen corporations created by the laws of Great Britain, but located on American soil, had, for years, impatiently endured violations of their charters by English rulers. The members of these corporations were British subjects, governed by laws made or sanctioned in England, and claiming the rights of British citizens. Clauses similar to the following occur in the charters of these corporations.

"All and every of the persons being our subjects, which shall dwell and inhabit within every or any of the said colonies . . . shall have and enjoy all liberties and franchises and immunities within any of our other dominions to all intents and purposes as if they had been abiding and born within this our realm of England."[1]

On the other hand, these corporations were as distinct and individual as are different railroad companies which have severally obtained charters and grants of land from the present government of the United States. The patent to Lord Baltimore, conferring upon him the territory of Maryland (1632), contains these significant words:

---

[1] Va. Charter of 1606. *Cf.* Dec. of Rights by Congress of 1774. Journals of Cong., I, 29.

"And further, our pleasure is . . . that the said province, tenants and inhabitants of the said colony or country shall not from henceforth be held or reputed as a member, or as part of the land of Virginia, or of any other colony whatsoever, now transported, or to be hereafter transported; nor shall be depending on or subject to their government in anything, from whom we do separate that and them. And our pleasure is, that they be separated, and that they be subject immediately to our crown of England as depending thereof forever."

As indicated by the provisions of which this paragraph is an example, the one relation common to all the colonies and colonists, was that of dependence upon the English crown and amenability to British law. The colony of Massachusetts Bay was as distinct from the colony of Pennsylvania as it was from the colony of Jamaica or the kingdom of Ireland. Had Virginia owed her allegiance to the crown of France, and Maryland her allegiance to the crown of Spain, they could not have been more mutually exclusive corporations, in all that pertained to regulation of their respective affairs. A British subject indeed, residing in one of these colonies, had the common law rights within the territory of the others. He had these rights, however, not as a member of another colonial corporation, but as a British citizen. He could exercise the right in the Bermudas or Barbadoes or Bengal as freely as in New Hampshire or New York or the Carolinas.

The attempts to secure recognition of common interests, and to obtain agreement upon plans of coöperation, beginning with the New England Confederation of 1643,[1] and ending with the flat failure of Franklin's scheme,[2] at the Albany Convention of 1754, prove that the colonists were far from readiness to merge their separate interests into those of a comprehensive

---

[1] For Art. of Confed. and Acts of the Commissioners of the United Colonies, *vid.* Plymouth Colony Records, Vols. IX and X.

[2] Text in Sparks's *Franklin*, I, 36. *Vid.* also Winsor, *Narrative and Critical Hist.*, V, 612; VI, 65-6.

organization. They refused to make such corporate recognition of mutual relations, as would be involved in the creation of organs for the performance of inter-colonial governmental functions.[1] The convention of 1765 further illustrates the growing need of concurrent action, but it would be difficult to demonstrate that, at this time, there had been progress towards willingness to adopt methods of concurrence which would in any way subject the action of single colonies to the dictation of the rest. The Congress of 1774 proved to be the introduction to inter-colonial coöperation.

Section II. The Composition of the Congress.

Who or what the Congress of 1774 represented, and what its powers were, can be decided by reference to the credentials of the members. We learn from these, in the first place, what parties of men sent the delegates.

"Monday, September 5, 1774, a number of the delegates, chosen and appointed by the several colonies and provinces in North America, to meet and hold a Congress at Philadelphia, assembled at the Carpenter's Hall."[2]   Of these, the delegates from New Hampshire, were chosen at a meeting "of the deputies" (85 in number) "appointed by the several towns."[3] The popular branch of the legislature appointed delegates or "committees,"[4] in Massachusetts, Rhode Island, and Pennsyl-

---

[1] Whether such organization could have been effected with the sanction of the home government, we need not enquire. The point is that the colonial corporations did not want such arrangement enough to take any effective steps towards it. That the British colonial office might have perfected a plan of consolidation for the benefit of the mother country is probable. That the colonists would have accepted it is questionable. The text of the English scheme appears in the New Jersey Archives, Ser. 1, vol. VIII, pt. II, p. 1, *sq.*

[2] J. of C., Ed. of 1823, Vol. I, p. 1.

[3] J. of C., I, 2.   [4] Mass. and Penn.

vania.[1] Connecticut was represented by a delegation selected by the colonial committee of correspondence, acting under instructions from the House of Representatives.[2] In New York City, delegates were chosen by popular vote in seven wards. The "committees of several districts" in different parts of the state accepted the representatives so determined upon as their own.[3] The county of Suffolk appointed a separate representative, and September 17, "a delegate from the county of Orange, in the colony of New York, appeared at Congress, and produced a certificate of his election by the said county."[4] King's county also chose a delegate who appeared in Congress October 1.[5] In New Jersey, "committees, appointed by the several counties,"[6] chose delegates. The language of the Delaware instructions is obscure; but it appears that "in pursuance of circular letters from the speaker of the house," "the representatives of the freemen of the government of the counties of New Castle, Kent, and Sussex, on Delaware," who would have constituted the Assembly, if regularly summoned, appointed delegates to the Congress.[7] In Maryland the selection was made "at a meeting of the committees appointed by the several counties of the province."[8] Virginia proceeded in the same manner.[9] In North Carolina, "a general meeting of deputies of the inhabitants" of the province took the responsibility of sending representatives.[10] In South Carolina, "a general meeting of the inhabitants" of the colony, nominated, appointed, and instructed "deputies," and the Commons House of Assembly resolved to "recognize, ratify and confirm the appointment."[11] Georgia was not represented.

It is obvious that a body so constituted was entirely extra-legal and irregular. It could have no authority to commit

---

[1] J. of C., I, 2 and 4. [2] J. of C., I, 3. [3] J. of C., I, 4.
[4] J. of C., I, 9. [5] J. of C., I, 15. [6] J. of C., I, 4.
[7] J. of C., I, 5. [8] J. of C., I, 6. [9] J. of C., I, 6.
[10] J. of C., I, 9. [11] J. of C., I, 7.

the colonial corporations to any course of action.[1] Even its significance as a reflector of popular opinion could only be approximately conjectured.

Section III. The Powers of the Members.

The credentials contain instructions appropriate, in nearly every case, to the extraordinary character of the Congress. The New Hampshire delegation were :

" To devise, consult, and adopt such measures, as may have the most likely tendency to extricate the colonies from their present difficulties; to secure and perpetuate their rights, liberties, and privileges, and to restore that peace, harmony, and mutual confidence, which once happily subsisted between the parent country and her colonies."[2]

The vote of the Massachusetts House reads :

" . . . do resolve; that a meeting of committees from the several colonies on this continent, is highly expedient and necessary, to consult upon the present state of the colonies, and the miseries to which they are and must be reduced, by the operation of certain acts of parliament respecting America, and to deliberate and determine upon wise and proper measures, to be by them recommended to all the colonies, for the recovery and establishment of their just rights and liberties, civil and religious, and the restoration of union and harmony between Great Britain and the colonies, most ardently desired by all good men. Therefore, resolved, that . . . be . . . a committee, on the part of this province, for the purposes aforesaid . . . "[3]

Governor Wanton, of Rhode Island, signed instructions as follows :

---

[1] In Mass., Conn., Penn., and especially R. I., there was apparently clearer legal authorization of the conference than in the other colonies. *Cf.* J. of C., I, 2.

[2] J. of C., I, 2.   [3] J. of C., I, 2.

" Whereas the general assembly of the colony aforesaid have nominated and appointed you . . . to represent the people of this colony in General Congress of representatives from this and other colonies. . . . I do therefore hereby authorize . . . you . . . to meet and join with the commissioners or delegates from the other colonies, in consulting upon proper measures to obtain a repeal of the several acts of the British parliament, for levying taxes upon his majesty's subjects in America, without their consent, and particularly an act lately passed, for blocking up the port of Boston, and upon proper measures to establish the rights and liberties of the colonies, upon a just and solid foundation. . . . "[1]

The Connecticut representatives were enjoined :

" To consult and advise on proper measures for advancing the best good of the colonies, and such conferences, from time to time, to report to this house."[2]

The New York delegates bore simply certificates of election as representatives of districts in the city, or counties.[3] In New Jersey, directions were issued :

" To represent the colony of New Jersey in the said General Congress,"[4]

The Assembly of Pennsylvania resolved :

" That there is an absolute necessity that a congress of deputies from the several colonies, be held as soon as conveniently may be, to consult together upon the present unhappy state of the colonies, and to form and adopt a plan for the purposes of obtaining redress of American grievances, ascertaining American rights upon the most solid and constitutional principles, and for establishing that union and harmony between Great Britain and the colonies, which is indispensably necessary to the welfare and happiness of both."[5]

The Delaware Assembly, assuming that as the governor had refused to summon the legislature in his other province of

---

[1] J. of C., I, 8.   [2] J. of C., I, 3.   [3] J. of C., I, 4.
[4] J. of C., I, 5.   [5] J. of C., I, 5.

Pennsylvania, he could not be expected to act otherwise in Delaware, declared that:

"The next most proper method of answering the expectations and desires of our constituents, and of contributing our aid to the general cause of America, is to appoint commissioners or deputies in behalf of the people of this government; to meet and act with those appointed by the other provinces, in General Congress: We do therefore . . . appoint . . . to consult and advise with the deputies of the other colonies, and to determine upon all such prudent and lawful measures, as may be judged most expedient for the colonies immediately and unitedly to adopt, in order to obtain relief for an oppressed people, and the redress of our general grievances."[1]

The committees appointed by the several counties of Maryland:

"Resolved, That . . . be deputies for this province, to attend a General Congress of deputies from the colonies, . . . to effect one general plan of conduct, operating on the commercial connection of the colonies with the mother country, for the relief of Boston, and preservation of American liberty."[2]

The delegates appointed from the different counties of Virginia, resolved:

"That it is the opinion of this meeting, that it will be highly conducive to the security and happiness of the British Empire, that a General Congress of deputies from all the colonies assemble as soon as the nature of their situations will admit, to consider of the most proper and effectual manner of so operating on the commercial connection of the colonies with the mother country, as to procure redress for the much injured province of Massachusetts Bay, to secure British America from the ravage and ruin of arbitrary taxes, and speedily to procure the return of that harmony and union, so beneficial to the whole empire, and so ardently desired by all British America." "The meeting proceeded to the choice of . . . for that purpose."[3]

---

[1] J. of C., I, 5.　　[2] J. of C., I, 6.　　[3] J. of C., I, 6.

The "general meeting of deputies of the inhabitants" of North Carolina, defined its purposes with more emphasis. It resolved :

" That we approve of the proposal of a General Congress, to be held in the city of Philadelphia, . . . to deliberate upon the present state of British America, and to take such measures as they may deem prudent, to effect the purpose of describing with certainty the rights of Americans, repairing the breach made in these rights, and for guarding them for the future from any such violations done under the sanction of public authority.

" Resolved, That . . . be deputies to attend such Congress, and they are hereby invested with such powers as may make any acts done by them, or consent given in behalf of this province, obligatory in honour upon every inhabitant hereof, who is not an alien to his country's good, and an apostate to the liberties of America."[1]

The Commons House of Assembly, of South Carolina, being informed that during the recess of the house

"a general meeting of the inhabitants" of the colony, appointed deputies "to meet the deputies of the other colonies of North America, in General Congress, . . . to consider the acts lately passed, and bills depending in parliament with regard to the port of Boston, and colony of Massachusetts Bay, which acts and bills, in the precedent and consequences affect the whole continent of America, also the grievances under which America labors, by reason of the several acts of parliament that impose taxes or duties for raising a revenue, and lay unnecessary restraints and burdens on trade; and of the statutes, parliamentary acts, and royal instructions, which make an invidious distinction between his majesty's subjects in Great Britain and America, with full power and authority to concert, agree to, and effectually prosecute such legal measures, as in the opinion of the said deputies, and of the deputies so to be assembled, shall be most likely to obtain a repeal of the said acts, and a redress of those grievances :

---

[1] J. of C., I, 9.

" Resolved, that this house do recognize, ratify, and confirm the appointment of the said deputies for the purposes mentioned."[1]

Such expressions as "prosecute such legal measures," in the South Carolina act; and the language of the last paragraph of the North Carolina instructions, have sometimes been used in support of the claim that the Congress thus constituted was more than a consultative and advisory body. It is, therefore, pertinent to analyze the proceedings of the Congress, in order to discover its own interpretation of its powers.

Section IV.   The Organization of the Congress of 1774.

After choice of President[2] and Secretary,[3] it was voted :

"That in determining questions in this Congress, each colony or province shall have one vote. The Congress not being possessed of, or at present able to procure proper materials for ascertaining the importance of each colony."[4]

September 5, 1774, the formation of committees began.   In the first place a committee, consisting of two from each of the colonies, was appointed :

"To state the rights of the colonies in general, the several instances in which these rights are violated or infringed, and the means most proper to be pursued for obtaining a restoration of them."[5]

A second committee was chosen, consisting of one delegate from each colony :

" To examine and report the several statutes, which affect the trade and manufactures of the colonies."[6]

September 27, it was resolved :

[1] J. of C., I, 7.   [2] Peyton Randolph, of Va.
[3] Charles Thomson, not a delegate.   [4] J. of C., I, 7.
[5] J. of C., I, 7, 8.   [6] J. of C., I, 7, 8.

"That from and after the 10th day of September, 1775, the exportation of all merchandise and every commodity whatsoever to Great Britain, Ireland, and the West Indies, *ought to* cease, unless the grievances of America are redressed before that time."

Whereupon it was ordered that a third committee of five members

"bring in a plan for carrying into effect the non-importation, non-consumption, and non-exportation resolved on."[1]

October 1, a committee of five was appointed to prepare "a loyal address to his majesty."[2] On the 7th, a committee of three was appointed :

"To prepare a letter to his excellency, general Gage, representing 'that the town of Boston and province of Massachusetts Bay are considered by all America as suffering in the common cause, etc.,' and entreating that the work of fortification be discontinued, 'and that a free and safe communication be restored and continued between the town of Boston and the country.'"[3]

October 11th, a committee of three was formed to prepare a "memorial to the people of British America," and "an address to the people of Great Britain."[4]

October 21st, a committee of three was appointed to prepare an address :

"To the people of Quebec, and letters to the colonies of St. John's, Nova Scotia, Georgia, East and West Florida, who have not deputies to represent them in this Congress."[5]

The committees thus enumerated are all, of any consequence, which the Congress appointed.

It seems superfluous to construe these facts. There was nothing administrative or governmental about the organization of the body. So far, it certainly did not exceed nor transgress the letter of its members' instructions.

---

[1] J. of C., I, 15. [2] J. of C., I, 16. [3] J. of C., I, 17.
[4] J. of C., I, 19. [5] J. of C., I, 38.

Section V. The Acts of the Congress of 1774.

In examining the acts of the first Congress, we are reduced
to an analysis of resolutions and pronunciamentos. The
various committees into which the body resolved itself received
certain instructions from the Congress,[1] which need not be
separately considered, as they were incorporated into the
reports subsequently submitted and accepted.

The Congress further received and considered several com-
munications. The most important of these were: First, an
account of the

" resolutions entered into by the delegates from the different towns
and districts in the county of Suffolk, in the province of Massachusetts Bay, on Tuesday, the 6th of September, and their address
to his excellency, governor Gage, dated the 9th." [2]

It does not appear that any specific action was expected of
the Congress, but the members resolved unanimously :

" That this assembly deeply feels the suffering of their countrymen in the Massachusetts Bay, under the operation of the late
unjust, cruel, and oppressive acts of the British parliament—that
they most thoroughly approve the wisdom and fortitude with
which opposition to these wicked ministerial measures has hitherto
been conducted, and they earnestly recommend to their brethren
a perseverance in the same firm and temperate conduct as
expressed in the resolutions, . . . trusting that the effect of the
united efforts of North America in their behalf, will carry such
conviction to the British nation of the unwise, unjust, and
ruinous policy of the present administration, as quickly to introduce better men and wiser measures.

" That contributions from all the colonies, for supplying the
necessities, and alleviating the distresses of our brethren at Boston,
ought to be continued in such manner and so long, as their occasions may require." [3]

---

[1] J. of C., I, 16, 17, *et passim.*   [2] J. of C., I, 9.   [3] J. of C., I, 14.

Whatever comment is necessary, by way of interpretation of these acts, with reference to the relations of which we are in search, may be made in connection with : Second, a letter from the Boston committee of correspondence, reciting the illegal and oppressive acts of the governor, and requesting "the *advice* of the Congress."[1] In response to this letter, the Congress, after appointing the committee mentioned above, resolved :

"That this Congress approve the opposition of the inhabitants of the Massachusetts Bay, to the execution of the late acts of parliament; and if the same shall be attempted to be carried into execution by force, in such case all America *ought to* support them in their opposition."[2]

The next day (October 10, 1774) Congress, resuming consideration of the same subject, resolved unanimously :

"That it is the opinion of this body, that the removal of the people of Boston into the country, would be not only extremely difficult in the execution, but so important in its consequences, as to require the utmost deliberation before it is adopted ; but in case the provincial meeting of the colony should judge it absolutely necessary, it is the opinion of the Congress, that all America ought to contribute towards recompensing them for the injury they may thereby sustain, and it will be recommended accordingly."

"*Resolved*, That the Congress recommend to the inhabitants of the colony of the Massachusetts Bay, to submit to a suspension of the administration of justice, where it cannot be procured in a legal and peaceable manner, under the rules of their present charter, and the laws of the colony founded thereon.

"*Resolved unanimously*, That every person and persons whomsoever, who shall take, accept, or act under any commission or authority, in any wise derived from the act passed in the last session of parliament, changing the form of government, and

---

[1] J. of C., I, 16.
[2] J. of C., I, 17. The Italics are mine.

3

violating the charter of Massachusetts Bay, *ought to* be held in detestation and abhorrence by all good men, and considered as the wicked tools of that despotism, which is preparing to destroy those rights, which God, nature, and compact have given to America."[1]

Surely no commentary could add to the conclusiveness of this language. It demonstrates that the body holding it was perfectly aware of its own character, as a committee of observation and recommendation, without legislative or executive powers of any sort.

On the 11th of October, the letter to Gen. Gage, prepared by the committee, was signed by the President, "in behalf of the General Congress." It recites, to be sure, that "the representatives of his majesty's faithful subjects in all the colonies from Nova Scotia to Georgia," have been appointed "the *guardians* of their rights and liberties."[2] But in this case, as almost invariably during the period, words must be interpreted by acts, or their import will be misunderstood. The protest to Gen. Gage, and the subsequent advice to the people of Massachusetts Bay, did not involve or imply any different relation of the Congress to the colonies from that which would exist between a committee of college students, protesting against alleged violation of laws of the trustees by some member of the faculty, and the general body of students, for whom, on the one hand, they spoke, and to whom they issued recommendations. Or, if a more perfect analogy be sought, a general convention of American railroad representatives, deliberating upon the rights and wrongs of their respective corporations under United States law, and on the one hand protesting to Congress against the administration of the Inter-State Commerce Act, and on the other hand, resolving upon advice to their principals, would illustrate the main fact in the relation between this Congress and the people by which it was created.[3]

---

[1] J. of C., I, 18.   [2] J. of C., I, 18.

[3] Of course no opinion upon the legal status of delegations, appointed as in 1774, is implied in this comparison.

Congress exemplified the nature of its function of guardianship again, by resolving unanimously, with reference to the people of Massachusetts Bay :

"That they be advised still to conduct themselves peaceably towards his excellency, general Gage, and his majesty's troops, now stationed in the town of Boston, as far as can possibly be consistent with their immediate safety, and the security of the town, avoiding and discountenancing every violation of his majesty's property, or any insult to his troops, and that they peaceably and firmly persevere in the line they are now conducting themselves, on the defensive."[1]

The most important business of the Congress was the preparation of the various documents which were intended not merely as weapons of peaceful warfare, but as incitement and equipment in case resort should be necessary to desperate means.

I. The first of these campaign documents was the *Declaration of Rights and Grievances.*[2] We must regard this composition as the chart which the Congress drew for its own guidance. It was the platform of the assembly. It was the congressional confession of faith. It contains the claims which were insisted on in America and disallowed in England until the alternative of submission or independence alone remained.[3]

---

[1] J. of C., I, 19.   [2] J. of C., I, 19–22.

[3] In the history of American political opinion this manifesto is a monument, but for the purposes of the present discussion, we need to notice only the fourth clause: "*Resolved*, That the foundation of English liberty, and of all free government, is a right in the people to participate in their legislative council: and as the English colonies are not represented, and from their local and other circumstances cannot properly be represented in the British parliament, they are entitled to a free and exclusive power of legislation in their several provincial legislatures, where the rights of representation can alone be preserved, in all cases of *taxation* and *internal polity*, subject only to the negative of their sovereign, in such manner as has been heretofore used and accustomed."

The words in Italics soon became familiar in state constitutions and elsewhere. Their meaning, like that of other familiar words of the period, must be derived from political not rhetorical usage.

II. The second measure of importance was the *Act of Association.*[1] The representatives of the twelve commonwealths signed an agreement containing a pledge to unite with the others to secure in each colony :

1. Non-importation from England, or English colonies not in the Association.

2. Discontinuance of the foreign slave trade.

3. Non-consumption of East India tea, and of certain other imports.

4. Non-exportation to England and colonies after September 5, 1775.

5. Regulations facilitating execution of the agreement.

6. Provision for improving the breed of sheep, and for equitable sale of mutton.

7. Encouragement of frugality and discouragement of luxury and extravagance.

8. Avoidance of scarcity prices and monopoly.

9. Prevention of evasion of this agreement by individuals.

10. Non-intercourse with "any colony or province in North America which shall not accede to, or which shall hereafter violate, this association," and determination to "hold them as unworthy of the rights of freemen, and as inimical to the liberties of their country."

11. Ratification of the assertion that: "We do solemnly bind ourselves and our constituents, under the ties aforesaid, to adhere to this association till the obnoxious acts are repealed.

The act concludes with the kind of provision which is the key to all acts of the Continental Congress :

"We *recommend* it to the provincial conventions, and to the committees in the respective colonies, to establish such farther

---

[1] J. of C., I, 23–26.

regulations as they may think proper, for carrying into execution this association."[1]

III. The third publication was an address to their "friends and fellow subjects" of Great Britain.[2] It is a review of the American case, at somewhat greater length and in more direct and persuasive language than in the Declaration of Rights. Appeal is taken from " wicked ministers and evil counsellors, whether in or out of office," to the magnanimity and justice of the British nation." It might have been issued with propriety by any patriotic individual, or by any single colony.[3] Weight attached to it beyond that which it would have possessed had it come from one of the latter sources, because it more obviously reflected the attitude of great numbers of the colonists. It was in no sense the announcement of a policy which a government was to force upon a people. It foreshadowed a policy according to which a people would presently find themselves obliged to extemporize a substitute for a government.

IV. The fourth expression of opinion worthy of notice is a memorial to the inhabitants of the twelve colonies.[4] It is

---

[1] It may not be superfluous to repeat that this epitome of the proceedings of the Congress is a rehearsal of familiar facts, with especial reference to obscured relations. The argument is: 1. The *powers* of the Congress, as defined by the votes of the bodies granting the credentials, are those of a committee for consultation and advice; 2. The *acts* of the Congress, which we are now analyzing, are conformable to these instructions; hence: 3. The authority of a "*government*" cannot be predicated of this committee.

If it be answered that no one now claims that the Congress of 1774 was in any sense a governmental body; the reply is that the same sort of reasoning which makes the Congress of 1775 a "national government," (vid. Curtis, Chap. II), might be applied to the Congress of 1774. If, therefore, the facts about this earlier committee of safety be recognized, the truth will be more readily perceived in the later case.

[2] J. of C., I, 26.

[3] Substantially this was done by South Carolina, September, 1775. Am. Archives, Ser. IV, Vol. III, 201; also by Mass., in the Spring of the same year. J. of C., I, 66-7.

[4] J. of. C., I, 31. It is worthy of note that Ga., because not represented in the Congress, was not mentioned among the colonies addressed.

another and wonderfully temperate discussion of the course of the British government from the close of the French war.   It announces the conclusion that:

" It is clear, beyond a doubt, that a resolution is formed, and now carrying into execution, to extinguish the freedom of these colonies, by subjecting them to a despotic government."

The Congress indicates, in most significant language, its true relation to the colonies, when it declares :

" Our resolutions[1] thereupon will be herewith communicated to you. But, as the situation of public affairs grows, daily, more alarming, and, as it may be more satisfactory, to you, to be informed by us, in a collective body, than in any other manner, of those sentiments that have been approved, upon a full and free discussion, by the representatives of so great a part of America, we esteem ourselves obliged to add this address to these resolutions."[2]

The memorial explains the considerations which prevailed in favor of the recommendation of commercial rather than military opposition to England, and concludes as follows :

" Your own salvation, and that of your posterity, now depends upon yourselves. You have already shown that you entertain a proper sense of the blessings you are striving to retain. Against the temporary inconveniences you may suffer from a stoppage of trade, you will weigh in the opposite balance the endless miseries you and your descendants must endure, from an established arbitrary power. You will not forget the honor of your country, that must, from your behavior, take its title in the estimation of the world, to glory, or to shame; and you will, with the deepest attention, reflect, that if the peaceable mode of opposition recommended by us be broken and rendered ineffectual, as your cruel and haughty ministerial enemies, from a contemptuous opinion of your firmness, insolently predict will be the case, you must inevit-

---

[1] Referring to the other acts mentioned in this section.
[2] J. of C., I, 32.

ably be reduced to choose either a more dangerous contest, or a final, ruinous, and infamous submission.

"Motives thus cogent, arising from the emergency of your unhappy condition, must excite your utmost diligence and zeal, to give all possible strength and energy to the pacific measures calculated for your relief: But we think ourselves bound in duty, to observe to you, that the schemes agitated against these colonies have been so conducted as to render it prudent, that you should extend your views to mournful events, and be, in all respects, prepared for every contingency. Above all things, we earnestly intreat you, with devotion of spirit, penitence of heart, and amendment of life, to humble yourselves and implore the favor of Almighty God ; and we fervently beseech his divine goodness to take you into his gracious protection."[1]

There is pathos, if not authority, in these words. The representatives of the colonies in Congress, from 1774 to 1783 were, all things considered, prudent and wise enough to have wielded vastly more power than they ever received. They were not a government, but their influence upon the different parties to the Association was exerted with patience and discretion which compel admiration. The weakness of the system by which the colonies coöperated makes more marvellous the persistency and resources of the men who, by use of that system, conquered success.

V. The fifth act to be mentioned in this connection is the resolution of October 22d :

" Resolved, *as the opinion of this Congress,* that it will be necessary that another Congress should be held on the tenth of May next, unless the redress of grievances, which we have desired, be obtained before that time. *And we recommend* that the same be held at the city of Philadelphia, and that all the colonies in North America choose deputies, as soon as possible, to attend such Congress."[2]

---

[1] J. of C., I, 38.   [2] J. of C., I, 39.

Attention to the italicised words will prevent attribution of authoritative character to the resolution.

VI. *The letter to the unrepresented colonies of St. John's, etc.*, approved October 22d, was but a brief note calling attention to the acts of the Congress, copies of which were enclosed, and recommending that the measures proposed be "adopted with all earnestness" by the colony addressed.[1]

VII. A vote which is usually passed over in silence, in accounts of this Congress, deserves to be included in this list: viz., the resolve of October 25, as follows:

"That this Congress, in their own names, and in behalf of all those whom they represent, do present their most grateful acknowledgments to those truly noble, honourable, and patriotic advocates of civil and religious liberty, who have so generously and powerfully, though unsuccessfully, espoused and defended the cause of America, both in and out of parliament."[2]

As the Congress possessed only moral powers, this apparently insignificant acknowledgment of friendship and sympathy in England was not only a deserved tribute to valuable allies, but it was the nearest approach to an actual evolution in the political battle that the character of the Congress permitted.

VIII. *The letter to the colonial agents* in England was a request that the authorized and recognized representatives of the colonial corporations, should act as media of communication between the extraordinary and irregular body claiming to speak for the corporations, and the king of Great Britain, and the other persons to whom the Congress sent addresses. It appealed to the personal zeal of the agents, as it could not command their official service, and expressed the hope that

"your good sense and discernment will lead you to avail yourselves of every assistance that may be derived from the advice and friendship of all great and good men who may incline to aid the cause of liberty and mankind." It also "begged the favor" that

[1] J. of C., I, 39.   [2] J. of C., I, 40.

the agents would " transmit to the speakers of the several assemblies the earliest information of the most authentic accounts you can collect, of all such conduct and designs of ministry or parliament as it may concern America to know."[1]

IX. *The address to the inhabitants of Quebec* was an olive branch to a people of another language and religion, between whom and the English colonists hardly concealed jealousies and suspicions existed ;[2] whose assistance would nevertheless be of no little consequence if the issues with the mother country should have to be decided by force. Although it seems to "talk down" to the people whose coöperation it was prepared to win, it is a spirited appeal to the French Catholics of Quebec, to resent the injuries and insults which they had received from the English government, and to seek reparation in alliance with their oppressed neighbors. It promised that the colonies for whom it spoke, although Protestant, would respect the religious convictions of the people of Quebec. It urged them to adopt the recommendations of the Act of Association. It invited them

" to add yourselves to us, to put your fate, whenever you suffer injuries which you are determined to oppose, not on the small influence of your single province, but on the consolidated powers of North America."[3]

It need hardly be remarked that all pledges and assurances in this document assumed the indorsement of the members of the twelve corporations for whom its authors spoke. That the indorsement would have been given is probable. That the Congress had any power to compel it need not be expressly denied.

---

[1] J. of C., I, 40.
[2] Vid. Declaration of the county of Suffolk, Art. 11. Also similar article in Dec. of Rights by the Congress.
[3] J. of C., I, 40–45.

X. The final important act of the Congress was the signing
of the *petition to the king*.[1] In the name and behalf of "his
majesty's faithful subjects" of the twelve colonies, it presented
another version of the same facts which had been so variously
proclaimed. It appeals from the ministers :

"Those designing and dangerous men, who daringly interposing
themselves between your royal person and your faithful subjects,
. . . have at length compelled us, by the force of accumulated
injuries, too severe to be any longer tolerable, to disturb your
majesty's repose by our complaints."[2]

Americans will probably never be able to account for the
stupidity of the English king, in refusing to be moved from
his fatal policy, in view of the matter in the complaints. It
is quite easy, however, to understand his displeasure at the
method and means of bringing the subject to his attention.
To use a modern term, the Continental Congress was an
inchoate "trust."   If Franklin's Albany proposition of 1754
had been considered dangerous by the home government, how
much more reason to fear even this federal advisory committee ![3]

Section VI.   The Corresponding Acts of the Colonies.

The same obscurity has not covered the relations between
the Congress of 1774 and the various colonies, which prevails
among commentators upon the character of the later Congresses.
It will, nevertheless, be well to recall a few typical acts of the
different colonial representative bodies, which will complete
our outline of congressional and colonial relations for the
period.

Although not in the strictest sense acts representing the
corporations, it is proper to mention the responses to the

---

[1] J. of C., I, 46–9.   [2] J. of C., I, 48.
[3] Vid. letter of Lord Dartmouth; Penna. Archives, 1st Ser., Vol. 4,
pp. 576–7.

recommendations of Congress, that Massachusetts be supported in her opposition to the oppressive acts of parliament, and that contributions be made to repair losses endured in the struggle.

The collections of the Massachusetts Historical Society contain the most satisfactory evidences that in each of the colonies there were people eager to observe and even anticipate the advice.[1] The letters referred to are full of information for the investigator of the tendencies of opinion in the colonies. They do not show, however, that the advice of the Congress had any marked influence on the contributors. Not only was aid sent before Congress met, but it would be difficult to prove that any more assistance was given than would have been rendered had Congress never mentioned the subject.

More directly indicative of popular sentiment, though at the same time confirmatory of the conclusion that the Congress was utterly devoid of coercive power, were the acts of popular gatherings, in view of the measures adopted by Congress.

In New Hampshire a popular convention, numbering one hundred and forty-four members, chosen by the towns, met, January 25, 1775, and declared its hearty approval " of the proceedings of the late grand continental Congress." The convention exhorted the people of New Hampshire " strictly to adhere to the Association."[2]

The provincial Congress of Massachusetts passed a resolve, December 5, 1774, approving the proceedings of Congress, and ordering a copy of the resolution to be sent to all the towns and districts.[3] Many of the inhabitants immediately signed a pledge to abide by the Association.

The Connecticut assembly unanimously approved the proceedings of the Congress, and ordered the towns to strictly observe the Association.

---

[1] Mass. Hist. Coll., Ser. IV, Vol. IV.

[2] N. H. Prov. Papers, Vol. VII, 443. The proceedings of several towns and counties appear, 444–51.

[3] Am. Archives, Ser. IV, Vol. I, 997, and J. of C., I, 50.

A special meeting of the Rhode Island assembly approved the proceedings of the Congress, December 8, 1774.[1]

In the New York Assembly the motion "to take into consideration the proceedings of the Continental Congress" was lost, and the empire state of the future stood with Georgia alone in a non-committal, and, it was feared, hostile attitude towards the measures recommended for relieving America from oppression.[2] The temper of New York was so doubtful that inquiry was set on foot in Virginia, March 24, 1775, as to whether the former colony had forsaken the colonial cause. The same question was agitated in Maryland and other colonies.[3]

The action of New Jersey, like that of nearly all the colonies, was at first fragmentary; but after various local ratifications,[4] the New Jersey delegates to the Continental Congress laid the proceedings of the continental body before the colonial assembly, October 24; and the house unanimously voted to approve the same, "such as are of the people called Quakers excepting only to such parts as . . . may have a tendency to force."[5] The provincial Congress of New Jersey resolved unanimously, May 26, 1775, to "earnestly recommend to the

---

[1] R. I. Col. Records, VII, 263.

[2] Am. Arch., Ser. IV, Vol. I, 1188–90. For resolves of counties, vid. same, *passim*.

[3] Am. Arch., Ser. IV, Vol. II, 1, 168, 379, 387, 389, 448. "New York was the pivot of the policy of ministers. Like North Carolina and Georgia, it was excepted from restraints imposed on the trade and fisheries of all the rest. The defection of its assembly from the acts of the general Congress was accepted as proof that it would adhere to the king; and the British generals, who were on the point of sailing for America, were disputing for the command at that place. . . . All believed that it had been won over to the royal cause, and that the other provinces could easily be detached, one by one, from the union, so that it would be a light task to subdue Massachusetts." Bancroft, IV, 149.

[4] Am. Arch., IV, I, 1028, 1051. N. J. Arch., Ser. I., Vol. X, 530. Am. Arch., IV, I, 1084, 1102, 1124.

[5] Am. Arch., IV, I, 1124, 1126, and letter of Gov. Franklin, N. J. Arch., I, 10, 575.

good people of this province, that they do most religiously adhere to the said resolution."[1]

The Pennsylvania Assembly approved the proceedings of the Congress, December 10, and recommended the good people to observe them inviolate.[2] The provincial convention confirmed this action the following January by voting unanimously :

"That this convention most heartily approve of the conduct and proceedings of the Continental Congress; that we will faithfully endeavor to carry into execution the measures of the Association entered into and recommended by them, and that the members of that very respectable body merit our warmest thanks by their great and disinterested labors for the preservation of the rights and liberties of the British colonies."[3]

In Delaware, the Assembly voted, March 15, 1775, "to approve of the proceedings of the late Congress."[4]

The counties of Maryland first chose committees "to carry into execution the Association agreed on by the American Continental Congress." Then a provincial meeting of deputies from the several counties, "read, considered, and unanimously approved" the proceedings of the Continental Congress (December 8-12). The convention further resolved :

"That every member of this convention will, and every person in the province ought, strictly and inviolably observe and carry into execution the Association agreed on by the said Continental Congress."[5]

"A convention of delegates for the counties and corporations" of Virginia met at Richmond, March 20, 1775, after many local ratifications had been voted, and resolved unanimously :

[1]Am. Arch., IV, II, 689.   [2]Am. Arch., IV, I, 1023.
[3]Am. Arch., IV, I, 1170.   [4]Am. Arch., IV, II, 126.
[5]Am. Arch., IV, I, 1031.

"That this convention doth entirely and cordially approve of the proceedings of the American Continental Congress."[1]

The House of Burgesses, June 5, 1775, adopted the following :

"Resolved, That this house doth entirely and cordially approve the proceedings and resolutions of the American Continental Congress, and that they consider this whole continent as under the highest obligations to that very respectable body, for the wisdom of their councils, and their unremitted endeavors to maintain and preserve inviolate the just rights and liberties of his majesty's dutiful and loyal subjects in America."[2]

The Assembly of North Carolina, April 7, 1775, passed the following resolve:

"That the house do highly approve of the proceedings of the Continental Congress, lately held at Philadelphia, and that they are determined, as members of the community in general, that they will strictly adhere to the said resolutions, and will use what influence they have to induce the same observance in every individual in this province."[3]

A provincial assembly had previously (August, 1774) promised to support the action of the Congress, and to have no further dealings with towns or individuals who declined to take similar action.[4]

After the vote of April 7, Governor Martin dissolved the Assembly (April 8, 1775).[5] At the same time and place a provincial convention was in session, and it voted (April 5) its approval of the act of association, and recommended to its "constituents" to adhere firmly to the same.[6] The provincial

---

[1] Am. Arch., IV, II, 167.   [2] Am. Arch., IV, II, 1192, 1221.
[3] J. of C., I, 54, and Am. Arch., IV, II, 265.
[4] Am. Arch., IV, I, 735.   [5] Am. Arch., IV, II, 266.
[6] Am. Arch., IV, II, 265 and 268.

Congress, which met August 21, 1775, ratified or repeated the approval.[1]

Deputies from every parish and district in South Carolina met (January 11, 1775) and voted "that this Congress do approve the American Association."[2]

Section VII.   Conclusions with Reference to Traditional Falla-cies about the Congress of 1774.

Comments upon typical expressions of opinion will suffi-ciently summarize the conclusions to be drawn from the facts thus far considered.

"*The signature of the Association by the members of Congress may be considered as the commencement of the American Union.*"[3]

"*The Association was virtually law, bearing on the individual. . . . the first enactment, substantially, of a general law by America.*"[4]

"*That memorable league of the continent in 1774, which first expressed the sovereign will of a free nation in America.*"[5]

If the words "union," "law," "sovereign," "nation," had not subsequently so often been forced on the rack of sophistry, to utter false evidence in justification of a theory, the expres-sions quoted might pass as natural and innocent hyperbole. They were not used hyperbolically by the school of interpreta-tion which prevailed until the close of the civil war, and which still holds its ground in the literature of our constitutional history. They were literal and exact technicalities, in conclu-sions, if not in premises. Composed into political creeds, these terms have been the means of exalting arbitrary and

---

[1] Am. Arch., IV. III, 186. The Mecklenburg Declaration is not referred to in this discussion, for reasons stated below. The last word on the subject has been well said in the *Magazine of American History*, for March, 1889, by President James C. Welling, LL. D.

[2] Am. Arch., IV, I, 1110–12.   [3] Hildreth, III, 46.

[4] Frothingham, *Rise of the Republic*, 373.

[5] President John Adams; Benton's Abridgment, II, 404.

unnatural hypotheses to the rank of fundamental truth. With
the endorsement of eminent names, they became the axioms of
a great political party, and the justification of a persistent,
and at length triumphant, political policy. Time will show
that the policy had more substantial justification than the
defective historical reasoning which supported it. Since the
end of a long historical process has been happily reached, it
is possible to examine calmly the views which contributed to
the result. Patriotic fictions are no longer political necessities. We shall not undermine or undervalue our present
nationality by showing that the philosophy which assisted in
its establishment was built on a misconception of history.

The term "union," then, can only by the most liberal
accommodation be used in connection with the agitations of
1774. There were common grievances. There was prospect
of remedy only in combination of the colonies for mutual
counsel and support. There was common indignation against
the mother country, with almost universal hope that reconcilia-
tion, not separation, would result. There was common determination to insist upon constitutional rights, and to grant moral
and material aid to the colony or colonies that might make
test cases with the home government. There was common
recognition of the necessity of coördinating effort under leadership competent to survey the whole situation and point out
suitable lines of action. There was common willingness to
adopt the advice of a central committee of observation. It
will be the aim of a later portion of this work to show that
all this, instead of being a matter of course, was evidence of
magnanimity altogether admirable. Concert only to this
extent was, in some respects, more difficult than it would be
to-day for all the republics of the Western Hemisphere to
form a commercial alliance. Concert to a greater extent cannot be created by theorizing after the event. To be proved, it
must be discovered. The records contain nothing beyond the
facts already characterized. To use the term "union," then,
with its present associations, is to introduce an inexcusable
historical solecism.

Of the word "law," similar assertions are necessary. There was no law, in any colony, but the constitution and laws of England, the special colonial charter, and the enactments of the legislative bodies which the charter authorized. The action of towns and counties upon the recommendations of the Congress, manifests the utmost uncertainty about the jurisdiction even of the local officers, and the sanction of the customary laws.[1]

It is a deliberate distortion of the instructions, the language and the acts of the Congress, and of the proceedings of the

---

[1] The relations of the local units to the earlier provincial assemblies cannot be discussed within the limits of this work. The subject deserves careful investigation in each State. Whether the relations which appear in the course of the year 1775, to be exhibited in the fifth section of Chapter III, are essentially new, or merely manifestations of what had previously been latent, I have purposely refrained from inquiring, because the question calls for thirteen distinct constitutional studies. The following citations simply fortify the statement in the text, without reference to further conclusions.

In case of N. H., Am. Arch., IV, I, 1105, 1229. The action of eastern Mass. need not be referred to specifically, as it is the substance of the Revolution thus far. In R. I., Am. Arch., IV, I, 1049. In Conn, same, 788, 827, 1038, 1075, 1215, 1202, 1236. In N. Y., same, 1027, 1035, 1068, 1091, 1100, 1164, 1183, 1191, 1201, 1230. In N. J., same, 1012, 1028, 1051, 1084, 1102, 1106, 1163. In Penn., same, 1052, 1144. In Va., same, 1008, 1022, 1026, 1031, and II, 281, 299, 372. In N. C. the resolves of the Committee of Mecklenburgh Co. (May 31, 1775, not the alleged declaration of the 20th), though belonging in the next period, deserve the most careful attention, Am. Arch., IV, II, 855. The following clauses are in place here:

"That all commissions, civil and military, heretofore granted by the crown, to be exercised in these colonies, are null and void, and the *constitution of each particular colony* wholly suspended.

"That the Provincial Congress of each province, under the direction of the great Continental Congress, is invested with all legislative and executive powers within their respective provinces, and that *no other legislative or executive power does, or can exist, at this time, in any of these colonies.*

"As all former laws are now suspended in this province, and the Congress have not provided others, we judge it necessary for the better preservation of good order, to form certain rules and regulations for the internal government of this county, until laws shall be provided for us by the Congress" (*i. e.*, the *provincial* Congress, as is evident from the context).

4

organizations that followed its advice, to represent it as, in any sense, a law-making body. Metaphor which can be so directly traced into fallacy deserves no toleration.

To admit the terms "sovereign," and "nation," into a description of American conditions at this stage, is to abandon investigation and classification, and to deliberately beg the issue. For the moment, government, even within the colonies, was partially paralyzed. It was doubtful who might command and who must obey. There is not a trace in any popular or official act of the time that can be rationally expounded as evidence of a claim, on the part of the Continental Congress, to power of inter-colonial control. Persons in South Carolina denounced Georgia, to be sure,[1] and there was talk of forcing that colony into participation with the rest. The argument was supposed expediency, justifying extraordinary action, not the assertion of any general principle subordinating the will of one colony to the command of all. The formation of a Continental Congress was the beginning of inter-colonial deliberation which broadened the horizon of the people, which emphasized the reasons for unity, which brought to popular attention the increasing number and importance of common interests, which created a continental opinion upon subjects of the most obvious common concern. The function of the first Continental Congress was not to express a "sovereign will," but to assist in the development of a common consciousness, so that there would, by and by, be a sovereign will to express. By creating this continental committee, the widely separated colonies became simply colonies testing the actuality and potency of their common ideas. They were no more a nation than twelve neighbors, meeting for discussion of a possible business venture, would be a partnership.

---

[1] Am. Archives, IV, I, 1163.

CHAPTER III.

THE CONGRESS OF 1775.[1]

Section I. The Parties Represented.

For the sake of clearness, although it involves repetition of reference and statement, the same lines of inquiry are here to be followed which have been observed in the preceding chapter. The people have, in almost every colony, committed themselves to revolution. They do not seem to realize that in discarding their charter governments they have decreed anarchy until they resort to the exercise of fundamental right and enact order. Wherever the charter government was no longer the *de facto* government; wherever the functions of government were performed under other sanction than that of the Crown of England, revolution was an accomplished fact. It required some time to teach the members of each colonial corporation this truth. Meanwhile the following organizations and bodies chose members of another continental committee, the character of which we shall discover by the same kind of examination as before.

In New Hampshire, "a convention of deputies appointed by the several towns in the province," met at Exeter, January 25, 1775, and chose two delegates.[2]

---

[1] Only the first session of this Congress, viz., from May 10 to August 1, will be treated in this chapter. Although in the Spring of 1776 a part of the delegates acted under new credentials, which will be noticed in the proper place, it is more convenient to group the facts of the second session of 1775 with those of the next year, including the early part of July.

[2] J. of C., I, 50.

In Massachusetts Bay, the Provincial Congress chose five representatives, December 5, 1774.[1]

In Rhode Island, the General Assembly chose two delegates, May 7, 1775.[2]

In Connecticut, the House of Representatives appointed five delegates, November 3, 1774.[3]

In New York, "a provincial convention, formed of deputies from the city and county of New York, the city and county of Albany, and the counties of Dutchess, Ulster, Orange, Westchester, King's, and Suffolk," with four representatives of certain free-holders of Queen's county, met, April 22, 1775, and appointed twelve delegates.[4]

In New Jersey, five delegates were chosen by the Assembly, January 24, 1775.[5]

In Pennsylvania, the Assembly appointed six deputies, December 15, 1774. Three others were added May 6, 1775.[6]

In Delaware, the Assembly chose three representatives, March 16, 1775.[7]

In Maryland, "a meeting of the deputies, appointed by the several counties of the province," chose, December 8, 1774, seven delegates, with liberty to "any three or more of them" to represent the colony.[8]

In Virginia, "a convention of delegates for the counties and corporations in the colony," elected seven delegates, March 20, 1775.[9]

In North Carolina, "a general meeting of delegates of the inhabitants of the province, in convention," April 5, 1775, appointed three delegates.[10]

The Assembly, two days later, approved the choice of the convention.[11]

---

[1] J. of C., I, 51.   [2] J. of C., I, 70.   [3] J. of C., I, 51.
[4] J. of C., I, 51. One half of these were evidently alternates.
[5] J. of C., I, 52.   [6] J. of C., I, 52.   [7] J. of C., I, 52.
[8] J. of C., I, 53.   [9] J. of C., I, 53.   [10] J. of C., I, 53.
[11] J. of C., I, 54.

In South Carolina, the Commons House of Assembly appointed five deputies, February 3, 1775.[1]

It would be foreign to our purpose to enter upon the question of the relation of these various delegations to the members of the colonial corporations for whom they were supposed to act.[2] Sufficient that revolution was strong enough to support these delegates, in each case, and to give them the authority of responsible agents of responsible principals.

Section II.   The Powers of the Members.

Variations, more or less striking in form, from the credentials of 1774, show, in the first place, that the parties sending representatives had more clearly defined purposes than before; but, in the second place, that they had not changed their views of the nature of the central committee, which was to further define their purposes and devise corresponding plans.

The New Hampshire delegates had authority as follows:

" To represent this province in the Continental Congress . . . and that they and each of them, in the absence of the other, have full and ample power, in behalf of this province, to consent and come to all measures, which said Congress shall deem necessary, to obtain redress of American grievances."[3]

The Massachusetts Bay delegation was

" appointed and authorized to represent this colony, on the tenth of May next, or sooner if necessary, at the American Congress, . . . with full power, with the delegates from the other American colonies, to consent, agree upon, direct, and order such further

---

[1] J. of C., I, 54. By a record on the same page, it appears that the "Provincial Congress of South Carolina" had previously "appointed and authorized" the same representatives.

[2] For illustration of the legal view of the question, vid. remarks of Gov. Campbell of S. C. Am. Arch., IV, II, 1044, 1618; also pp. 7, 236, 253-4, 273, 1547.

[3] J. of C., I, 50.

measures as shall to them appear to be best calculated for the recovery and establishment of American rights and liberties, and for restoring harmony between Great Britain and the colonies."[1]

The Rhode Island representatives were instructed:

"To represent the people of this colony in a general Congress of representatives, from this and the other colonies, . . . there, in behalf of this colony, to meet and join with the commissioners or delegates from the other colonies, in consulting upon proper measures to obtain a repeal of the several acts of the British parliament, for levying taxes upon his majesty's subjects in America, without their consent; and upon proper measures to establish the rights and liberties of the colonies upon a just and solid foundation, agreeable to the instructions given you by the general assembly."[2]

The Connecticut delegates were:

"Authorized and empowered to attend said Congress, in behalf of this colony, to join, consult, and advise with the delegates of the other colonies in British America, on proper measures for advancing the best good of the colonies."[3]

The New York delegates held commission:

"To represent this colony at such Congress, with full power . . . to meet the delegates from the other colonies, and to concert and determine upon such measures as shall be judged most effectual for the preservation and reëstablishment of American rights and privileges, and for the restoration of harmony between Great Britain and the colonies."[4]

The New Jersey delegation was appointed:

"To attend the Continental Congress of the colonies, . . . and report their proceedings to the next session of general assembly."[5]

---

[1] J. of C., I, 51.   [2] J. of C., I, 70.   [3] J. of C., I, 51.
[4] J. of C., I, 52.   [5] J. of C., I, 52.

The Pennsylvania representatives were :

"Appointed deputies on the part of this province to attend the general Congress, . . . and that they or any four of them do meet the said Congress accordingly, unless the present grievances of the American colonies shall, before that time, be redressed."[1]

The credentials of the Delaware delegation contained authorization :

"To represent this government at the American Congress, . . . with full power to them or any two of them, together with the delegates from the other American colonies, to concert and agree upon such further measures as shall appear to them best calculated for the accommodation of the unhappy differences between Great Britain and the colonies, on a constitutional foundation, which the house most ardently wish for, and that they report their proceedings to the next sessions of general assembly."[2]

To the Maryland delegates, authority was given :

"To represent this province in the next Continental Congress ; . . . and that they, or any three or more of them, have full and ample power to consent and agree to all measures, which such Congress shall deem necessary and effectual to obtain a redress of American grievances, and this province bind themselves to execute, to the utmost of their power, all resolutions which the said Congress may adopt. And further, if the said Congress shall think necessary to adjourn, we do authorize our said delegates, to represent and act for this province, in any one Congress, to be held by virtue of such adjournment."[3]

The Virginia credentials simply certified that the persons named in them were chosen :

"To represent this colony in general Congress, to be held at the city of Philadelphia on the tenth day of May next."[4]

---

[1] J. of C., I, 52.   [2] J. of C., I, 52.   [3] J. of C., I, 53.
[4] J. of C., I, 53.

The North Carolina representatives presented at Philadelphia certificates that they were:

"Invested with such powers as may make any acts done by them, or any of them, or consent given in behalf of this province, obligatory, in honor, upon every inhabitant thereof."[1]

The credentials given by the South Carolina Commons House of Assembly, appointed:

". . . deputies, for and in behalf of this colony, to meet the deputies appointed, or to be appointed, on the part and in behalf of the other colonies, . . . with full power and authority to concert, agree to, and effectually prosecute such measures as, in the opinion of the said deputies, and the deputies to be assembled, shall be most likely to obtain a redress of American grievances."[2]

The credentials of the Provincial Congress to the same individuals read:

". . . appointed and authorized to represent this colony, . . . at the American Congress, . . . with full power to concert, agree upon, direct, and order such further measures as, in the opinion of the said deputies, and the delegates of the other American colonies to be assembled, shall appear to be necessary for the recovery and establishment of American rights and liberties, and for restoring harmony between Great Britain and her colonies."[3]

Massachusetts, Maryland, North Carolina, and South Carolina use, in these credentials, expressions which, taken by themselves, might be understood to delegate more power than the Congress ever exercised. On the other hand, the instructions of Rhode Island, New Jersey, Pennsylvania, neither express nor imply any definite purpose to be guided by the

---

[1] J. of C., I, 53. In this connection it is worthy of note that the Provincial Congress of N. C. voted credentials, September 2, 1775, for representatives to the Congress of September 5, or later, in which, after the words "in behalf of this province," the clause is inserted, "not inconsistent with such instructions as may be given by this Congress." Am. Arch., IV, III, 195.
[2] J. of C., I, 54.   [3] J. of C., I, 54.

decisions of the Congress. Taken as a whole, the credentials seem to create a body of counsellors, whose deliberations were likely to be so wise that the results would be accepted by the colonies in general as guides of their conduct. If Massachusetts and South Carolina intended to obey the *orders* of the Congress, they were certainly alone in expressing such intentions. If Maryland really meant to pledge compliance with all the recommendations of the Congress, there is certainly food for reflection in the fact that Maryland was the last colony of all to ratify the Articles of Confederation, and that the other states were on the point of forming a confederation without her, when she gave her consent to the proposal of Congress, more than three years after it was made, and nearly two years after all the other states had voted to accept the articles.[1]

According to the canons of interpretation observed in the case of the first Congress, it is necessary to subject these credentials to comparison with the acts of the body which the accredited persons composed. It is certain that the powers voted and attested by the documents here cited, received no increments from the journey to Philadelphia. The language of the credentials meant no more when read in Congress than when voted in the several colonies. The body which organized in Philadelphia plainly had no powers over and above the sum of the powers authorized in the twelve sets of instruc-

---

[1] J. of C., II, 610–18, III, 135–6, 201, 280, 281, 283, 576, 592. In the proper place it will be shown that Maryland deserved the gratitude of Americans for stoutly maintaining her position in respect to Western lands. The above allusion has simply this bearing: Argument from the language of the Maryland credentials, that henceforth Maryland was subject to the determinations of the Continental Congress, is estopped by the recorded and famous fact that Maryland was most conspicuously independent of such determinations. This is but another illustration of the principle contended for throughout this work, viz.: the character of institutions, and the nature of relations must be discovered by examination of the institutions and relations themselves, not merely of the language which occasioned or recognized their existence.

tions. Adding together twelve authorizations to "consult and advise," could not make power to command. The Congress may use its position in one of three ways : it may, first, simply debate, reach expressions of the opinion of the majority, transmit the same to the colonies, and await their action ; it may, second, resolve upon active measures, and take the first steps in carrying them into execution, depending upon the colonies to endorse its proceedings ; it may, third, assume governmental control of the people of the colonies, and attempt to establish the prerogative of forcible coercion of the constituencies represented.

The first form of procedure would be in accordance with the most restricted interpretation that could possibly be placed upon the instructions ; the second course would exceed the letter of some of the instructions, but it might fairly be held to correspond with the apparent intent of the greater number, and to be in violation of no express or certainly implied restriction of any ; the third possible line of conduct would have only the single word "order," in the Massachusetts Bay and South Carolina resolves, as explicit authorization.

If the first possibility were found to be the actual course of Congress, that body would evidently be merely a committee of advisers, and nothing more. If the second possibility be found realized in congressional acts, the body is then a committee, not only of consultation, but of leadership. If the third possibility be the historical reality, the body which acted for the colonies was a board of government, and the twelve coöperating corporations were a commonwealth under central control, instead of twelve self-determining and self-governing communities.

We have now to examine the records to discover which of the three hypothetical possibilities was actualized.

Section III.   The Organization of the Congress of 1775.

May 10, 1775, Peyton Randolph was unanimously chosen president, and Charles Thomson was, also by a unanimous vote, appointed secretary. A door-keeper and a messenger were, at the same time, selected, and it was agreed to invite one of the city clergymen to act as temporary chaplain." [1]

May 13, Lyman Hall presented himself with credentials from the parish of St. John's, Georgia, and requested admission to the Congress.[2] He was admitted as a delegate from the parish of St. John's, "subject to such regulations as the Congress shall determine, relative to his voting."[3]

The first committee of which mention is made in the Journals, was formed May 15, "to consider what posts are necessary to be occupied in the colony of New York," and "to report as speedily as possible." [4] Congress was practically, thus far, in continual committee of the whole, " to take into consideration the state of America." [5] The differentiation of functions in committees can hardly be said to have begun earlier than June 14th.[6] Besides the committee mentioned above, another of three members, was appointed May 26th, to prepare and bring in a letter to the people of Canada ;[7] another, May 27th, " to consider on ways and means to supply these colonies with ammunition and military stores;[8] another, May 29th, "to get the letter " (to Canada) " translated into the French language, . . . printed, . . . and dispersed among the inhabitants there;"[9] another " to consider the best means of establishing post for conveying letters and intelligence through this continent;" [10] and on June 3d, six committees were formed, for the following purposes :

(*a*) to consider the letter from the convention of Massachusetts, dated the 16th May, "and report what, in their opinion, is the proper advice to be given to that convention ; "

---

[1] J. of C., I, 50.

[2] His papers explain the situation in Ga. J. of C., I, 68.

[3] J. of C., I, 67.   [4] J. of C., I, 70.

[5] J. of C., I, 67, 71, 72, 73, 74, 77, 78, 79, 80, 82, 83.

[6] J. of C., I, 83. It might be placed much later.

[7] J. of C., I, 74.   [8] J. of C., I, 74.   [9] J. of C., I, 76.

[10] J. of C., I, 76.

(*b*) " to draught a petition to the king ; "

(*c*) " to prepare an address to the inhabitants of Great Britain ; "

(*d*) " to prepare an address to the people of Ireland ; "

(*e*) " to bring in the draught of a letter to the inhabitants of Jamaica ; "

(*f*) " to bring in an estimate of the money to be raised." [1]

June 8, a committee was instructed to examine the papers of one Skene, a prisoner in the custody of the Philadelphia troops, and reported to be " a dangerous partizan of administration," with " authority to raise a regiment in America." It was voted :

" That the said committee be upon honor to conceal whatever of a private nature, may come to their knowledge by such examination, and that they communicate, to this Congress, what they shall discover, relative to the present dispute, between Great Britain and America." [2]

In addition to these committees, one was formed June 7, to draft a " resolution for a fast ; " [3] another, June 10, to devise ways and means to introduce the manufacture of salt-petre in these colonies ; " [4] another, June 14, " to prepare rules and regulations for the government of the army ; " [5] another, June 16, " to draught a commission and instructions for the general ; " [6] another, on the same day, " to report what steps, in their opinion, are necessary to be taken for securing and preserving the friendship of the Indian nations ; " [7] another, June 19, " to prepare the form of a commission for the major-generals, also for the brigadier-generals, and other officers in the army ; " [8] another, June 23, to draw up a declaration, to be published by General Washington, upon his arrival at the camp before Boston ; [9] another, the same day, " to get proper

[1] J. of C., I, 79.   [2] J. of C., I, 80.   [3] J. of C., I, 79–81.
[4] J. of C., I, 81.   [5] J. of C., I, 83.   [6] J. of C., I, 84.
[7] J. of C., I, 84.   [8] J. of C., I, 86.   [9] J. of C., I, 88.

plates engraved, to provide paper, and to agree with printers
to print" the bills of credit;[1] another, June 24, "to devise
ways and means to put the militia of America in a proper
state for the defence of America;"[2] another, July 21, "to
superintend the press, and to have the oversight and care of
printing the bills of credit ordered to be struck by this Congress."[3]

With a few unimportant exceptions, the above is a full list
of the congressional committees, up to the adjournment, August
1. Criticism of the functions provided for in this organization may properly be reserved until the acts performed by the
Congress have been considered.

Section IV. The Acts of the Congress of 1775.

As details now begin to claim the attention of the Congress,
its acts must be grouped, and only the most important representative measures particularly noticed. The business of the
Congress with which this inquiry is concerned, was:

1. *To dispose of sundry applications, on behalf of individuals.*
These were all, apparently, cases that arose under the non-
intercourse provisions of the Association. In the case of
Robert and John Murray, desiring to be restored to their
former situation with respect to their commercial privileges,
while the form of expression used by Congress implies that
its answer was an authoritative permission, the resolve was in
fact a formulation of the principle which, in the opinion of
Congress, the spirit of the Association required the local committees to observe. The answer was:

"That where any person hath been or shall be adjudged by a
committee, to have violated the continental association, and such
offender shall satisfy the convention of the colony, where the
offence was or shall be committed, or the committee of the parish
of St. John's, in the colony of Georgia, if the offence be committed

[1] J. of C., I, 88.　　[2] J. of C., I, 88.　　[3] J. of C., I, 121.

there, of his contrition for his offence, and sincere resolution to
conform to the association for the future; the said convention, or
committee of the parish of St. John's aforesaid, may settle the
terms upon which he may be restored to the favor and forgiveness
of the public, and that the terms be published."[1]

The fact that such subjects could be dealt with, under exist-
ing circumstances, by local authorities alone, and that Congress
had no jurisdiction in the premises, could not have been more
plainly recognized, if it had been expressly asserted.

2. *To consider requests for advice and aid to individual
colonies.* May 3, 1775, the Provincial Congress of Massachusetts Bay directed to Congress a request for "direction and
assistance."[2] It urges the need of a powerful army to oppose
"the sanguinary zeal of the ministerial army," and to end the
"inhuman ravages of mercenary troops." The petitioners
add :

" We also inclose several resolves for empowering and directing
our receiver-general to borrow the sum of one hundred thousand
pounds, lawful money, and to issue his notes for the same; it
being the only measures, which we could have recourse to, for
supporting our forces, and we request your assistance in rendering
our measures effectual, by giving our notes a currency throughout
the continent."

The papers referred to included a series of affidavits, by
eye-witnesses and participants, correcting false accounts of the
affairs of Concord and Lexington ;[3] and an address from the
Watertown Provincial Congress of Massachusetts Bay to the
inhabitants of Great Britain.[4]

On the second of June another request of similar, yet in
some respects more weighty, import, was received from the

---

[1] J. of C., I, 74. For other cases, vid. pp. 70 and 134.
[2] J. of C., I, 56, *sq.*   [3] J. of C., I, 58–66.   [4] Same, 66–7.

same Provincial Congress.[1] The resolution of Congress, in response to these requests, has furnished material for a vast deal of inconsequent argumentation. Comments upon it may be deferred till further facts have been cited. The text was as follows:

" Resolved, That no obedience being due to the act of parliament for altering the charter of Massachusetts Bay, nor to a governor, or a lieutenant-governor, who will not observe the directions of, but endeavor to subvert, that charter, the governor and lieutenant-governor of that colony are to be considered as absent, and their offices vacant; and as there is no council there, and the inconveniences, arising from the suspension of the powers of government, are intolerable, especially at a time when general Gage hath actually levied war, and is carrying on hostilities, against his majesty's peaceable and loyal subjects of that colony; that, in order to conform, as near as may be, to the spirit and substance of the charter, it be recommended to the provincial convention, to write letters to the inhabitants of the several places, which are entitled to representation in assembly, requesting them to chuse such representatives, and that the assembly, when chosen, do elect councillors; and that such assembly, or council, exercise the powers of government, until a governor, of his majesty's appointment, will consent to govern the colony according to its charter."[2]

May 13, " a petition from the county of Frederick, in Virginia, addressed to the Congress, was presented and read."[3] May 15, " the city and county of New York having, through the delegates of that province, applied to Congress for advice how to conduct themselves with regard to the troops expected

---

[1] It urged the Congress " to favour them with explicit advice respecting the taking up and exercising the powers of civil government," and declared their readiness " to submit to such a general plan as the Congress may direct for the colonies, or make it their great study to establish such a form of government there, as shall not only promote their advantage, but the union and interest of all America." J. of C., I, 78.

[2] June 9, 1775. J. of C., I, 80.   [3] J. of C., I, 69.

there, the Congress took the matter into consideration,"[1] and
"recommended, for the present, to the inhabitants of New York,
that if the troops, which are expected, should arrive, the said
colony act on the defensive, so long as may be consistent with
their safety and security; that the troops be permitted to remain
in the barracks, so long as they behave peaceably and quietly,
but that they be not suffered to erect fortifications, or take any
steps for cutting off the communication between the town and
country, and that if they commit hostilities or invade private
property, the inhabitants should defend themselves and their
property, and repel force by force; that the warlike stores be
removed from the town; that places of retreat, in case of necessity, be provided for the women and children of New York, and
that a sufficient number of men be embodied, and kept in constant
readiness for protecting the inhabitants from insult and injury."[2]

A single illustration of another class of applications will
suffice. June 14, "a letter from the convention of New York,
dated 10th instant, respecting a vessel which is stopped there,
on suspicion of having on board provisions for the army and
navy at Boston, was read and referred to the delegates of
Massachusetts Bay, Connecticut, and New York."[3] The
next day it was voted to send the following answer to the
chairman of the New York convention:

"Resolved, That the thanks of this Congress be given to the
convention of New York, for their vigilance in the case of capt.
Coffin's vessel, and that it be recommended to them that the vessel
be unloaded, and the cargo safely stored, until all just suspicions,
concerning the destination of it, shall be removed."[4]

3. *To act as the mouthpiece of the patriotic party in all the
colonies.* The Congress appeared in this character when, July
6, 1775, it agreed to the "Declaration by the Representatives
of the United Colonies of North America, now met in Congress at Philadelphia, setting forth the causes and necessity of

---

[1] J. of C., I, 69.   [2] J. of C., I, 70.   [3] J. of C., I, 83.
[4] J. of C., I, 83.

their taking up arms." In tracing the progress of political opinion, this document must be carefully compared with the "Declaration of Rights and Privileges" by the first Congress.[1] Each of these deserves to constitute a chapter in all hand books of American history.

A few expressions in the later document should be noticed in our present inquiry. The paper declares: "Our cause is just. *Our union is perfect.*"[2]

The contention of this argument is that the idea conveyed to the people of the time by the word "union," and the fact which alone existed as the correlate of that word, must be sought in contemporary interpretations, either formal or practical. In this instance the idea is developed in the protestation:

"With hearts fortified with these animating reflections, we most solemnly, before God and the world, declare, that, exerting the utmost energy of those powers which our beneficent Creator hath graciously bestowed upon us, the arms we have been compelled by our enemies to assume, we will, in defiance of every hazard, with unabating firmness and perseverance, employ for the preservation of our liberties, being with one mind resolved to die freemen rather than live slaves."[3]

The "union" of the time then, was the common purpose to postpone all minor interests in prosecuting this determination. The inter-colonial coöperation, which prudence dictated, in no recognized sense committed the colonies to any system of permanent relations, after the object for which they temporarily combined had been attained. "Union" was, at this period, a concept with which the notion of fixed, organic connection had not yet been joined.

4. *To serve as an organ of communication between the collective colonies and other communities or individuals.* May 29, an address to "the oppressed inhabitants of Canada" was adopted.

In behalf of the united colonies, the Congress argued with the "friends and countrymen," "fellow-subjects," and "fellow-sufferers" of Canada, that the "fate of the Protestant and Catholic colonies" was "strongly linked together." The letter expressed condolence with the Canadians on account of their deprivation of freedom by the home government, and professed confidence that they "will not, by tamely bearing the yoke, suffer pity to be supplanted by contempt." It characterized, in terms intended to rouse the indignation of the Canadians against England, the tyranny to which, in both civil and religious matters, the people of Canada had been subjected, and the degradation which submission to such despotism involved. It renewed the assurances of friendship made by the Congress of 1774, and called upon the Canadians to join the other colonies "in the defence of our common liberty," and especially in "imploring the attention of our sovereign, to the unmerited and unparalleled oppressions of his American subjects," that he may "at length be undeceived,' and forbid a licentious ministry any longer to riot in the ruins of the rights of mankind."[1]

July 8, the Congress adopted an address to the inhabitants of Great Britain.[2] It claims to be a second attempt to interest "friends, countrymen, and brethren" of England, in preventing the dissolution of ties which bind Englishmen in America with those at home. It is a strong, clear, candid presentation of facts in addition to those which had been reviewed in the first address. It demands no further remark in this connection.

The address to the King of Great Britain,[3] adopted also June 8, though remarkable for its profuse expressions of loyalty, and the conciliatory, yet dignified tone of its plea for relief, adds nothing which requires mention here.

The address to the "lord mayor, aldermen, and livery of

---

[1] J. of C., I, 74-6.   [2] J. of C., I, 106.   [3] J. of C., I, 104.

London," [1] contains thanks " for the virtuous and unsolicited resentment shown to the violated rights of a free people ; " a declaration that " North America wishes most ardently for a lasting connection with Great Britain on terms of just and equal liberty ; " and an assurance that while determined to defend themselves " like the descendants of Britons," the Americans still hope " that the mediation of wise and good citizens will prevail over despotism, and restore harmony and peace, on permanent principles, to an oppressed and divided empire." These last three addresses were, as in the similar cases of the preceding year, sent to Mr. Richard Penn, and the colony agents in London, with the request that they be immediately presented. [2]

The address to the Assembly of Jamaica is a rapid account of the reasons which compelled the colonies to include the British West India Islands in the non-intercourse agreement. [3]

The import of the address to the people of Ireland, [4] may be gathered from the opening paragraph :

" Friends and Fellow-Subjects !

"As the important contest, into which we have been driven, is now become interesting to every European state, and particularly affects the members of the British empire, we think it our duty to address you on the subject. We are desirous, as is natural to injured innocence, of possessing the good opinion of the virtuous and humane. We are peculiarly desirous of furnishing you with a true state of our motives and objects; the better to enable you to judge of our conduct with accuracy, and determine the merits of the controversy with impartiality and precision."

Near the end of the address is a sentence whose optimism is noteworthy, yet as pointed out in a similar case above, it is entirely anachronistic to interpret the language as indicative of organized nationality :

---

[1] J. of C., I, 111.   [2] J. of C., I, 112.   [3] J. of C., I, 122.
[4] July 28, 1775. J. of C., I, 125.

" *Blessed with an indissoluble union,* with a variety of internal resources, and with a firm reliance on the justice of the Supreme Dispenser of all human events, we have no doubt of rising superior to all the machinations of evil and abandoned ministers."[1]

In the acts thus enumerated there is implied no suggestion of any change in the relations between the Congress and the colonies, since acts of like character were performed in 1774.

5. *To devise peaceful plans and measures for the general good.* Of this class the examples arc very numerous. May 17, the Congress voted unanimously :

" That all exportations to Quebec, Nova Scotia, the island of St. John's, Newfoundland, Georgia, except the parish of St. John's, and to East and West Florida, immediately cease, and that no provision of any kind, or other necessaries be furnished to the British fisheries on the American coasts, until it be otherwise determined by the Congress."[2]

When it is remembered that the enforcement of such a resolution depended entirely upon the determination of the towns, counties, or colonies, according to the condition of organization in each province at the time; and that it actually was enforced by local authorities, not by the Congress; the baselessness of the claim that the Congress exerted a sovereign power in the premises, is apparent.

May 29, the colonial committees were earnestly recommended to prevent the exportation (except from Massachusetts Bay) of provisions or necessaries of any kind to the island of Nantucket. This was to shut off a source of supply for English fishermen.[3] June 1, it was voted that :

"As this Congress has nothing more in view than the defence of these colonies, *Resolved,* That no expedition or incursion ought to be undertaken or made, by any colony, or body of colonists, against or into Canada; and that this resolve be immediately transmitted to the commander of the forces at Ticonderoga."[4]

[1] J. of C., I, 128.   [2] J. of C., I, 71.   [3] J. of C., I, 76.
[4] J. of C., I, 77.

June 2, it was resolved :

" That no bill of exchange, draught, or order of any officer in the army or navy,[1] their agents or contractors, be received or negotiated, or any money supplied to them by any person in America; that no provisions or necessaries of any kind be furnished or supplied to, or for the use of, the British army or navy, in the colony of Massachusetts Bay ; that no vessel employed in transporting British troops to America, or from one part of North America to another, or warlike stores or provisions for said troops, be freighted or furnished with provisions or any necessaries, until further orders from this Congress." [2]

June 10, the towns and districts in the northern colonies were "recommended " to collect as much salt-petre and brimstone as possible, and send it to the provincial convention at New York.[3] The said convention was "recommended" to put the powder mills in order for the manufacture of all such materials.[4] Like action was urged upon the southern colonies.[5]

June 12, the Congress issued a proclamation, earnestly recommending to the inhabitants of the colonies the observance of Thursday, the 20th of July, "as a day of public humiliation, fasting, and prayer." [6] Whether any importance may be attached to the change or not, it is curious that the first two fast day proclamations were addressed directly to the people of the colonies; but after the Declaration of Independence the legislatures of the several states were recommended to appoint both fast and thanksgiving days.[7]

July 4, Congress resolved :

" That the two acts passed in the first session of the present parliament," for restraining the trade and commerce of the colonies, were " unconstitutional, oppressive, and cruel, and that the

---

[1] British.
[2] J. of C., I, 78.
[3] J. of C., I, 81.
[4] J. of C., I, 81.
[5] J. of C., I, 81.
[6] J. of C., I, 81.
[7] J. of C., I, 576, II, 309, 469, III, 125, 229, 377, 441, 537.

commercial opposition of these colonies, to certain acts enumerated in the association of the last Congress, ought to be made against these, until they are repealed."[1]

July 12, Congress organized a systematic superintendence of Indian affairs for the colonies. Three departments were created: the northern, middle, and southern. Five commissioners were assigned to the southern, and three to each of the other two departments. The commissioners were empowered:

"To treat with the Indians in their respective departments, in the name, and on behalf of the united colonies, in order to preserve peace and friendship with the said Indians, and to prevent their taking any part in the present commotions."[2]

Congress elected the commissioners for the northern and middle departments,[3] and two of the five for the southern department.[4] The remaining three were left to the council of safety of South Carolina.[5]

July 15, Congress adopted the following preamble and resolution:

"Whereas, the government of Great Britain hath prohibited the exportation of arms and ammunition to any of the plantations, and endeavored to prevent other nations from supplying us; 'Resolved, That for the better furnishing these colonies with the necessary means of defending their rights, every vessel importing gun-powder, salt-petre, sulphur, provided they bring with the sulphur four times as much salt-petre, brass field-pieces, or good muskets fitted with bayonets, within nine months from the date of this resolution, shall be permitted to load and export the produce of these colonies, to the value of such powder and stores aforesaid, the non-exportation agreement notwithstanding; and *it is recommended to the committees of the several provinces* to inspect the military stores so imported, and to estimate a generous price for the same, according to their goodness, and permit the importer of

---

[1] J. of C., I, 99.   [2] J. of C., I, 113.   [3] J. of C., I, 117.
[4] J. of C., I, 120–121.   [5] J. of C., I, 120.

such powder and other military stores aforesaid, to export the value thereof and no more, in produce of any kind.' " [1]

One of the most timely and sagacious acts of this Congress, was the formulation, July 31, of the principles at issue between the colonies and the home government. In February of that year the English House of Commons had passed a resolve as follows :

" That when the general council and assembly, or general court of any of his majesty's provinces, or colonies in America, shall propose to make provision, according to the condition, circumstance, or situation of such province or colony, for contributing their proportion to the common defence (such proportion to be raised under the authority of the general court, or general assembly of such province or colony, and disposable by parliament) and shall engage to make provision also, for the support of the civil government, and the administration of justice in such province or colony, it will be proper, if such proposal shall be approved by his majesty, and the two houses of parliament, and for so long as such provision shall be made accordingly, to forbear in respect to such province or colony, to lay any duty, tax, or assessment, except only such duties as it may be expedient to continue to levy or impose for the regulation of commerce ; the net produce of the. duties last mentioned to be carried to the account of such province or colony respectively." [2]

It would be difficult to imagine a more cunning proposition of ostensible concessions by the home government. Acceptance of them by an American colony would have been tacit surrender to all the claims against which the Americans were in revolt. Some of the colonies might have been caught in the snare if there had been no common council. The Congress scarcely appears to better advantage than in furnishing the colonies a platform upon which to unite in repelling such disingenuous advances.

---

[1] J. of C., I, 118.   [2] J. of C., I, 131.

The parliamentary resolution having been referred to Congress by the assemblies of New Jersey, Pennsylvania, and Virginia, a reply was adopted which exposes the subtlety of the English proposal, and furnishes one of the most statesmanlike justifications of the American demands, in the whole series of revolutionary declarations. In such work as this the service of the Congress to the colonial cause was inestimable. The proposal is pronounced " unreasonable and insidious."

"Unreasonable because, if we declare we accede to it, we declare without reservation, we will purchase the favor of parliament, not knowing at the same time at what price they will please to estimate their favor; it is insidious, because individual colonies, having bid and bidden again, till they find the avidity of the seller too great for all their powers to satisfy, are then to return into opposition, divided from their sister colonies whom the minister will have previously detached by a grant of easier terms, or by an artful procrastination of a definitive answer."[1] The opinion continues: "Upon the whole, this proposition seems to have been held up to the world, to deceive it into a belief that there was nothing in dispute between us but the mode of levying taxes; and that the parliament having now been so good as to give up this, the colonies are unreasonable if not perfectly satisfied: Whereas, in truth, our adversaries still claim a right of demanding *ad libitum*, and of taxing us themselves to the full amount of their demand, if we do not comply with it. This leaves us without anything we can call property. But, what is of more importance, and what in this proposal they keep out of sight, as if no such point was now in contest between us, they claim a right to alter our charters and establish laws, and leave us without any security for our lives or liberties."[2]

The last measure of this class which need be mentioned, was the establishment of a postal system. The exercise of power of this character has been made much of, in arguments upon the political character of the Congress. The fact that an inter-

---

[1] J. of C., I, 132.   [2] J. of C., I, 133.

colonial postal system grew naturally into a department of national administration, need not, however, obscure the fact that its origination was a measure rather of revolutionary than of civil policy, and that in the institution of such a service, Congress was acting in its capacity of temporary committee of safety, by virtue of authorization, the nature of which will be further illustrated as we proceed. This is evident by the content of the resolution constituting the committee on the subject:

"As the present critical situation of the colonies renders it highly necessary that ways and means should be devised for the speedy and secure conveyance of intelligence from one end of the continent to the other, Resolved, That . . . be a committee to consider the best means of establishing post for conveying letters and intelligence through this continent."[1]

The subsequent establishment of "a line of posts, under the direction of the post-master general, from Falmouth in New England, to Savannah in Georgia, with as many cross posts as he shall think fit,"[2] is thus properly classed with plans for rendering the resistance of the colonies more effective.

6. *To devise offensive and defensive measures to be urged upon the individual colonies.* Thus, in view of the British design of invading the colonies from Quebec, the capture of Ticonderoga was approved (May 18, 1775), and Congress

"earnestly recommended it to the committees of the cities and counties of New York and Albany, immediately to cause the said cannon and stores to be removed from Ticonderoga to the south end of lake George; and, if necessary, to apply to the colonies of New Hampshire, Massachusetts Bay, and Connecticut, for such an additional body of forces as will be sufficient to establish a strong post at that place, and effectually to secure said cannon and stores, or so many of them as it may be judged proper to keep there."[3]

---

[1] May 29, 1775. J. of C., I, 76.   [2] July 26, 1775. J. of C., I, 124.
[3] J. of C., I, 72.

Again (May 20, 1775) it was resolved unanimously :

"That the militia of New York be armed and trained, and in constant readiness to act at a moment's warning; and that a number of men be immediately embodied and kept in that city, and so disposed of as to give protection to the inhabitants, in case any insult should be offered by the troops, that may land there, and prevent any attempts that may be made to gain possession of the city, and interrupt its intercourse with the country."[1]

It was also voted unanimously the same day:

"That it be recommended to the provincial convention at New York, to persevere the more vigorously in preparing for their defence, as it is very uncertain whether the earnest endeavors of the Congress, to accommodate the unhappy differences between Great Britain and the colonies, by conciliatory measures, will be successful."[2]

May 30, it was resolved :

"That the governor of Connecticut be *requested* immediately to send a strong reinforcement to the garrisons of Crown Point and Ticonderoga ; " "that the president acquaint governor Trumbull, that it is the *desire* of Congress, that he should appoint a person, in whom he can confide, to command the forces at Crown Point and Ticonderoga;" "That the provincial convention of New York be . . . *desired* to furnish " the troops at those posts " with provisions and other necessary stores, and to take effectual care that a sufficient number of batteaus be immediately provided for the lakes;" and "that it be *recommended* to the government of Connecticut, or the general of the forces of that colony, to appoint commissaries to receive at Albany and forward the supplies of provisions, for the forces on lake Champlain, from the provincial convention of New York, and that the said convention use their utmost endeavors in facilitating and aiding the transportation thereof, from thence to where the said commissaries may direct."[3]

---

[1] J. of C., I, 73.   [2] J. of C., I, 73.   [3] J. of C., I, 77.

Recommendations were sent to various parts of the continent urging the people to collect and send to central points all available sulphur and saltpetre.[1] The provincial convention of New York was "desired immediately to apply to governor Trumbull to order the Connecticut troops, now stationed at Greenwich, Stanford, and parts adjacent, to march towards New York."[2]

June 19, the letters from Massachusetts Bay being taken into consideration, the Congress came to the following resolve:

" That the governor of Connecticut be requested to direct all the forces raised in that colony, not employed at Ticonderoga and Crown Point, or recommended by this Congress to be marched towards New York, to be immediately sent to join the combined army before Boston; and it is earnestly recommended to the colony of Rhode Island, and to the provincial convention of New Hampshire, to send immediately to the army before Boston, such of the forces as are already embodied, towards their quotas of the troops agreed to be raised by the New England colonies."[3]

June 22, it was resolved:

" That the colony of Pennsylvania raise two more companies of riflemen, and that these, with the six before ordered to be by them raised, making eight companies, be formed into a battalion, to be commanded by such field officers, captains, and lieutenants, as shall be recommended by the assembly or convention of said colony."[4]

The next day it was resolved:

" That it be recommended to the convention of New York, that they, consulting with general Schuyler, employ in the army to be raised for the defence of America, those called Green Mountain Boys, under such officers as the said Green Mountain Boys shall chuse."[5]

---

[1] J. of C., I, 81.   [2] June 16. J. of C., I, 85.
[3] J. of C., I, 86.   [4] J. of C., I, 87.   [5] J. of C., I, 88.

June 26, the state of North Carolina being taken into consideration, the Congress came to the following resolutions :

"Whereas it is represented to this Congress, that the enemies of the liberties of America are pursuing measures to divide the good people of the colony of North Carolina, and to defeat the American association, Resolved, That it be recommended to all in that colony, who wish well to the liberties of America, to associate for the defence of American liberty, and to embody themselves as militia, under proper officers.

" Resolved, That in case the assembly or convention of that colony shall think it absolutely necessary, for the support of the American association and safety of the colony, to raise a body of forces not exceeding one thousand men, this Congress will consider them as an American army, and provide for their pay." [1]

A resolve was passed, July 1 :

" That in case any agent of the ministry, shall induce the Indian tribes, or any of them, to commit actual hostilities against these colonies, or to enter into an offensive alliance with the British troops, thereupon the colonies ought to avail themselves of an alliance with such Indian nations as will enter into the same, to oppose such British troops and their Indian allies." [2]

July 18, Congress resolved :

" That it be recommended to the inhabitants of all the United English Colonies in North America, that all able bodied effective men, between sixteen and fifty years in each colony, immediately form themselves into regular companies of militia." [3]

It was voted the same day :

" That it be recommended to the assemblies or conventions in the respective colonies to provide, as soon as possible, sufficient stores of ammunition for their colonies; also that they devise proper means for furnishing with arms, such effective men as are poor and unable to furnish themselves."

---

[1] J. of C., I, 89.   [2] J. of C., I, 98.   .   [3] J. of C., I, 118.

It was voted further :

"That it be recommended to each colony to appoint a committee of safety, to superintend and direct all matters necessary for the security and defence of their respective colonies, in the recess of their assemblies and conventions;" and further, "that each colony, at their own expense, make such provision by armed vessels or otherwise, as their respective assemblies, conventions, or committees of safety shall judge expedient and suitable to their circumstances and situations, for the protection of their harbors and navigation on their sea-coasts, against all unlawful invasions, attacks, and depredations, from cutters and ships of war."[1]

It was resolved, and such resolutions became very frequent in a short time :

"That it be recommended to the colonies of New Hampshire, Massachusetts Bay, Rhode Island, and Connecticut, to complete the deficiencies in the regiments belonging to their respective colonies, retained by the general in the continental army before Boston;" also "that it be recommended to the colony of Rhode Island to complete and send forward to the camp before Boston, as soon as possible, the . . . men lately voted by their general assembly."[2]

7. *To raise, organize, and regulate a continental army, and assume general direction of military affairs.* On the 14th of June, it was resolved: "That six companies of expert riflemen, be immediately raised in Pennsylvania, two in Maryland, and two in Virginia;" that each company, as soon as completed, march and join the army near Boston, to be there employed as light infantry, under the command of the chief officer of that army.[3] A scale of pay was adopted;[4] a form of enlistment was promulgated;[5] the grades of officers were

---

[1] J. of C., I, 119.
[2] The identical resolution, the number of men excepted, was passed with reference to Conn. J. of C., I, 120.
[3] J. of C., I, 82. [4] J. of C., I, 82–3–4–7, 129. [5] J. of C., I, 83.

fixed upon, and the number in certain grades determined;[1] officers of the higher grades were appointed by the Congress;[2] a hospital staff was organized;[3] and elaborate rules were drawn up for the government of the army.[4] On the 15th of June Washington was unanimously "appointed to command all the continental forces raised, or to be raised, for the defence of American liberty."[5] After the form of his commission had been agreed upon, June 17, it was resolved unanimously, ". . . this Congress doth now declare, that they will maintain and assist him, and adhere to him, the said George Washington, with their lives and fortunes in the same cause."[6]

Such records as the following indicate the relation of Congress to the movements of the army:

"The Congress then resumed the consideration of affairs in the New-York department, and after some time spent therein, came to certain resolutions, which were ordered to be immediately transmitted to general Schuyler for his direction."[7]

"Resolved, That general Schuyler be empowered to dispose of and employ all the troops in the New York department, in such manner as he may think best for the protection and defence of these colonies, the tribes of Indians in friendship and amity with us, and most effectually to promote the general interest, still pursuing, if in his power, the former orders from this Congress, and subject to the future orders of the Commander in chief."[8]

"Resolved, That a body of forces, not exceeding five thousand, be kept up in the New York department, for the purpose of defending that part of America, and for securing the lakes, and protecting the frontiers from incursions or invasions."[9]

8. *To create and administer a continental revenue.* The signal for the beginning of that financial policy which afterwards

---

[1] J. of C., I, 84.   [2] J. of C., I, 85–6, 120.   [3] J. of C., I, 124.
[4] J. of C., I, 90–98.   [5] J. of C., I, 83.
[6] J. of C., I, 85. Other instructions to Washington appear under date June 20, in the Secret Journals of Cong., Vol. I, p. 17. Ed. of 1821.
[7] J. of C., I, 89.   [8] July 20, 1775. J. of C., I, 120.
[9] J. of C., I, 123. July 25.

exerted so nearly a decisive influence upon the formation of permanent interstate relations, was given, June 22, in the resolution :

"That a sum not exceeding two million of Spanish milled dollars be emitted by the Congress in bills of credit, for the defence of America."[1]

On the 29th of July, it was voted :

"That each colony provide ways and means to sink its proportion of the bills ordered to be emitted by this Congress, in such manner as may be most effectual and best adapted to the condition, circumstances and equal mode of levying taxes in such colony."

"That the proportion or quota of each colony be determined according to the number of inhabitants, of all ages, including negroes and mulattoes in each colony."[2]

"That each colony pay its respective quota in four equal annual payments,"[3] and that for this end, the several provincial assemblies, or conventions, provide for laying and levying taxes in their respective provinces or colonies, towards sinking the continental bills; that the said bills be received by the collectors in payment of such taxes, &c."[4]

The same day (July 29) it was resolved :

"That Michael Hillegas, and George Clymer, esqrs., be joint treasurers of the United Colonies; that the treasurers reside in Philadelphia, and that they shall give bond, with surety, for the faithful performance of their office, in the sum of one hundred thousand dollars."

---

[1] J. of C., I, 87–8.

[2] An arbitrary apportionment was made to guide until a census could be taken. J. of C., I, 130. In a later section the acts of the separate colonies in making this paper legal tender, providing penalties for counterfeiting, &c., will be cited in exposure of the fallacy of the claim that the Congress was here exercising "one of the highest acts of sovereignty."

[3] *I. e.* in terms ending Nov., 1779, 1780, 1781, and 1782. J. of C., I, 130.

[4] The resolutions of the provincial Congress of New York (May 30, 1775), on the subject of continental revenues, should be compared at this point. Am. Arch., IV, II, 1254, 1262.

" That the provincial assemblies or conventions do each choose a treasurer for their respective colonies, and take sufficient security for the faithful performance of the trust." [1]

In illustration of the manner and purpose of disbursements, at this time, the votes of the last day of the session may be cited :

" Resolved, That the sum of five hundred thousand dollars, be immediately forwarded from the continental treasury, to the paymaster general, to be applied to the use of the army in Massachusetts-Bay, in such manner, as general Washington, or the commander in chief for the time being, by his warrants, shall limit and appoint; and if the above sum shall be expended before the next meeting of the Congress, then that general Washington, or the commander in chief for the time being, be empowered to draw upon the continental treasury, for the sum of two hundred thousand dollars, in favor of the paymaster general, to be applied for the use and in the manner above mentioned." [2]

A similar appropriation was made for the use of General Schuyler in the New-York department.[3] It was also voted :

" That a sum not exceeding one hundred and seventy-five thousand dollars be paid to the provincial convention of New-York, to be applied towards the discharge of the moneys advanced and the debts contracted for the public service, by the said provincial convention and the committee of Albany, in pursuance of the directions of this Congress ; and that the said provincial convention account to this Congress, at their next meeting, for the application of the said money." [4]

A resolution of the same nature was passed in favor of the colony of Connecticut.[5] It was further resolved :

" That the sum of sixteen thousand dollars be paid to the delegates of the colony of Pennsylvania, in full for the like sum by them borrowed by order of the Congress, on the 3d of June last,

---

[1] J. of C., I, 130.   [2] J. of C., I, 134.   [3] J. of C., I, 135.
[4] J. of C., I, 134.   [5] J. of C., I, 135. .

for the use of the continent;"[1] and "That the sum of ten thousand dollars be placed in the hands of the delegates of Pennsylvania, or any three of them, for contingent services, and that out of the same, be paid the expenses incurred for raising and arming the rifle companies, and for expresses and other small charges, of which the Congress have not been able to procure exact accounts; and that the said committee do lay before the Congress, at their next meeting, an account of their proceedings in that matter."[2]

Section V. Conclusions.

This review justifies the following conclusions upon the questions raised at the end of the last section. The Congress of 1775 was not content with mere expression of opinions. It took a large view of its powers. It realized that its efficiency depended wholly upon the acceptance of its acts by the principals of the different delegations; but, following its judgment as to what the patriotism of the colonies would approve and sustain, it initiated action of various kinds, which, from the beginning, assumed the certainty of adoption by the colonies, and derived all its energy from the probability of such ratification. The Congress doubtless exceeded the letter of the instructions received by a portion of its members; but this was not from any misconception of those instructions, nor from any uncertainty about the essentially advisory character even of those of its proceedings which appeared most peremptory. In pointing out to the colonies the direction which their preparations for resistance ought to take, the Congress no more acted upon an imagined authority to *command* the colonies, than does the lookout at the bow of the ship, when he reports the direction of danger to the officer of the deck. The Congress unquestionably enjoyed a prestige at this juncture, which it subsequently lost. The people, and even the provincial conventions, occasionally addressed it in a tone which indicated that they unconsciously attributed to it power which it plainly did not possess.

---

[1] J. of C., I, 135.   [2] J. of C., I, 135.

It would be easy to collate a long array of expressions from the votes of the Congress, which show that its language was influenced, to a certain extent, towards the assumption of an importance inconsistent with its real power. Nothing could be more natural, inasmuch as, under the circumstances, whatever the Congress decided or recommended the colonies were almost sure to adopt. The prestige of such influence could hardly fail to mould advice sometimes into the semblance of requirement. I am unable to find a single evidence, however, that the members ever entertained a doubt about their actual subordination to the colonial assemblies which they represented.

As the provincial congresses grew more accustomed to their position, and as intercourse with the Continental Congress exhibited the limitations of the latter in a thousand examples, all parties began to understand the precise character of the continental body, and its relation to the States. Resistance would be impotent unless it was concerted.[1] The Congress was the only possible medium of coördination and combination. It was the clearing-house of colonial news and opinion. The situation, resources, temper, strength and weakness of the protesting communities could nowhere be so advantageously considered ; nor could the disposition of their available means of defence be so prudently made from any other position. In adopting recommendations that came from such vantage ground, the colonies were sure of directing their operations by the utmost strategic and economic wisdom.

Or again, the Congress was the central office of a coöperative political signal service. Its bulletins were enacted into rules by the colonial assemblies, not because they were recognized as statutes, but because they were accepted as the most accurate readings of the signs of the times. The storm, to be averted if possible, or to be breasted if necessary, was just breaking upon different sections of the country. The Congress could

---

[1] This idea was well expressed in resolutions of citizens of Savannah, June 13, 1775. Am. Arch., IV, II, 1544.

best calculate its course and its character, and could best suggest precautions and expedients.

The Congress was a sagacious committee of safety. It knew the minds of the people it acted for. It knew the occasions for action. It knew the possibilities of action. It knew what demands could be made and it made them ; not as a legislative chamber would make them, but as popular leaders, who had the ear of the colonial assemblies. Its calls for the mobilization of the militia were enforced by the fact that there was work for the militia to do, and by the assurance involved in the calls that the colonies would collectively assume the responsibility incurred by any individual colony in undertaking the work. Its creation of a continental army was a sensible "straight cut" to the association of forces, implying nothing whatever about permanent relations of Congress to colonies.[1] It was made possible simply by the expressed or tacit assent of each colony to the temporary omission of formalities taken for granted in the whole proceeding. Its issuance of bills of credit was banking upon the public spirit of the colonial corporations. As agents holding indefinite powers of attorney, the delegates pledged the credit of their principals. All the power they had for such a purpose had been created in the colonies, and by the colonies, and could be authoritatively interpreted and actually exerted only by the parties giving it. The pledge of the credit of a colony by its delegation was not the source of the colony's obligation, but the colony entered into an obligation by authorizing or endorsing its delegates' pledge. In a word, the Congress of 1775 did no act by any power other than that which the separate corporations repre-

---

[1] I mean by this that the colonists did not consciously commit themselves to any form of organization, or to any permanent relationship of an organized interstate character, by allowing the Congress thus to act for the whole. A philosophical view of their experience discovers in the very naturalness of such an arrangement the foreshadowing of a permanent organ of similar action. The people had not, however, willed the establishment of the future order.

sented individually contributed. It was a Congress of deputies, not of legislators. Its executive operations were vicarious,
not functional. It performed no single act which did not
derive viability from sustentation by the local powers. Its
history forms a record of localism rising superior to itself, to
meet the demands of a crisis. That imagination runs riot
which turns this magnificent effort into the definitive abdica-
tion of localism. The last time the proposal of centralization
was formally broached, it was rejected.[1] Not constitution
building but constitution saving was the object now. The
colonies combined not to substitute one dependence for another,
but to make their relation to England one of independence.[2]
In the freedom of that further actual independence which
English policy had made the only alternative with submission,
the colonial corporations created a medium of common offence
and defence in which localism did not expire, but in which
localism displayed its maximum possibilities for resistance
and aggression.

These conclusions will be confirmed by considering the same
set of relations from the opposite point of view.

Section VI.   The Corresponding Acts of the Colonies.

The people of the several colonies were meanwhile adopting
temporary organizations for the control of their corporate
affairs. These organizations, or their successors, inherited or
usurped all the prerogatives which had belonged to the charter
organizations. The people gradually recognized them as the
organs of popular rights of self-government, sanctioned therefore by a law superior to that of the constitution. The people
did not at first have definite and unanimous opinions about the

---

[1] Albany Congress of 1754.

[2] *I. e.* in the sense in which the word was used in the earliest discussions;
independence of unconstitutional parliamentary or ministerial dictation.
Vid. Am. Arch., IV, II, 1548–9; and same, 21.

respective spheres of town, county and colonial authorities; but it is true in general that, wherever such a change in form was necessary, the provincial congress assumed the executive and legislative position from which the governor and the charter legislature were displaced. The fact to be placed over against the description of the general Congress is that the people of the separate colonies acquiesced in the assumption and exercise, by their provincial assemblies, of every essential power of government. The evidence of this is next in order. Its importance in the argument will appear at a later stage of the investigation.[1]

---

[1] The evidence which I have arranged chronologically on this point, in the case of each of the thirteen colonies in turn, justifies certain generalizations irreconcilable with the traditional views of inter-colonial relations at this period. It establishes the fact that *the colonial authorities looked to the Continental Congress not for sanctions, in the legal sense, but for signs.* The evidence to this effect becomes more and more decisive as we approach July, 1776.

At the end of the next chapter this body of evidence will be discussed as a whole; *first,* in its bearing upon the conclusion just indicated; *second,* with reference to its bearing upon the constitutional significance of the Declaration of Independence. The details to be placed in evidence, with respect to the independent action of the individual colonies, are so numerous that the argument must be interrupted at this point, to be resumed in a future number of the Studies.